New Directions in Fair Isle Knitting

New Directions in Fair Isle Knitting

Patty Knox

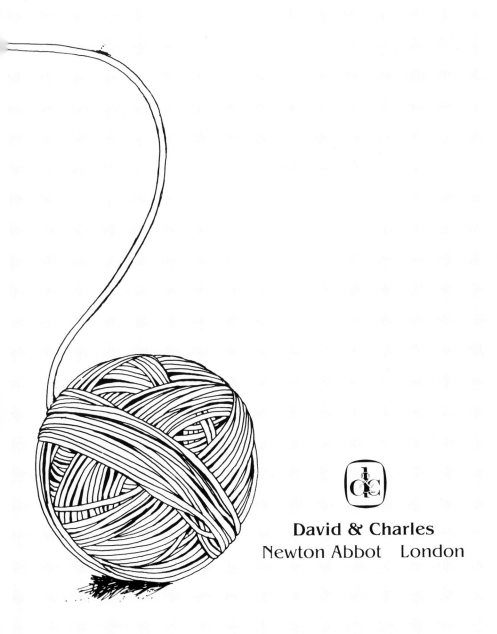

David & Charles
Newton Abbot   London

Acknowledgements

Photography by Tony Griffiths, Photography 2000
Many thanks to: Pam Griffiths
Charlotte Knox for the line drawings and illustrations
Flora Samuel for her help with the diagrams and colour graphs
Elizabeth Shellswell and Sue Hopper for their help with the knitting instructions
The knitters who were so ably organised by Elizabeth – Mrs Debenham, Frances,
Gwen, Gill, Heather, Helen, Lesley, Olive, Pat, Viola and Winifred
Sue Hopper (again) for the chapters on Techniques and Machine Knitting
and Coral Mula for the illustrations
Jamieson & Smith (SWB) Ltd of Lerwick, Shetland Isles, for their most courteous
and prompt service
Last but not least acknowledgement to Tim and Olly (wool winders)

British Library Cataloguing in Publication Data

Knox, Patty
   New directions in Fair Isle knitting.
   1. Knitting – Scotland – Fair Isle – Patterns
   I. Title
   646.4'07   TT819.S35

   ISBN 0-7153-8619-0

Phototypeset by Typesetters (Birmingham) Ltd,
Smethwick, West Midlands
and printed in The Netherlands
by Smeets Offset BV, Weert
for David & Charles (Publishers) Limited
Brunel House   Newton Abbot   Devon

Contents

Wavelets   38
V neck pullover

Jellyfish   40
V neck pullover

Bunny Rabbits   42
jumper

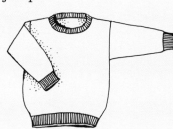

Planes   44
jumper

Coco   47
cardigan

Pansy   50
V neck jumper

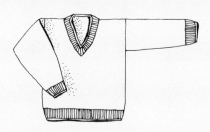

Bumble Bees   53
round neck pullover

Butterflies   56
V neck pullover

Zigzag   59
pullover, cap & scarf

Caterpillars   62
V neck pullover

Mushrooms   65
V neck pullover

Strawberries   68
waistcoat

Tottie   71
V neck jumper

Charity   74
baggy pullover

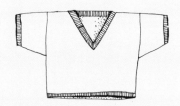

Waves   76
V neck pullover

Checkers 78
V neck pullover

Sissy Pink 81
V neck pullover

Darts 84
waistcoat

Fall 87
waistcoat

Flower Pots 90
V neck pullover

Inca 92
V neck sweater

Fir Trees 95
waistcoat

Gardener's Garters 98
legwarmers

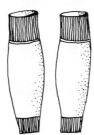

Woolly Bag 100

Techniques

More Knitting Know-How

Mushrooms cardigan & bootees

Pattern repeat 8 sts and 65 rows

Sizes
To fit 40[46]cm (16[18]in) chest.
Length 18[23]cm (7[9]in).
Sleeve seam 14[16]cm (5½[6½]in).

Materials
1 skein of Shetland 2 ply wool in main colour (beige).
1 skein each of 8 contrast colours (brick red, airforce blue, dusky pink, rust, light green, cinnamon, white, donkey brown).
Pair 2¾mm (No 12) needles.
Pair 3¼mm (No 10) needles.
2.50mm (No 12) crochet hook.
4 small buttons.

Tension
30 sts and 34 rows to 10cm (4in) over patt worked on 3¼mm needles.

BACK AND FRONTS (worked in one piece to armholes)
With 2¾mm needles and 1st contrast (rust) cast on 116[132] sts.
Work 1 row K1, P1 rib.
Change to main colour (beige) and work 5 more rows in rib.
Change to 3¼mm needles.
1st size only
Beg with the 9th row of chart, work in patt for 32 rows (row 40 on chart).
2nd size only
Beg with 1st row of chart, work in patt for 40 rows.

Shape neck (both sizes)
Keeping patt correct, work 2 tog, work to last 2 sts, work 2 tog. Work one row.

Divide for armholes
Next row: Work 2 tog, patt across 27[35] sts for right front, turn leaving rem sts on holder.
Keeping armhole edge straight, cont dec at neck edge every alt row until

18[20] sts rem.
Cont without shaping until the 66th [74th] row of chart has been worked. Cast off.
Rejoin yarn to rem sts and patt across 56[64] sts for back, turn and leave rem sts on holder.
Keeping armhole edges straight work in patt until back measures same as for front shoulder edge.
Cast off 18[20] sts at beg of next 2

rows. Leave rem sts on holder.
Rejoin yarn to sts for left front and complete to match right front reversing all shaping.

SLEEVES
With 2¾mm needles and first contrast (rust) cast on 40[46] sts.
Work 1 row K1, P1 rib.
Change to main colour (beige) and work 10 more rows in rib.

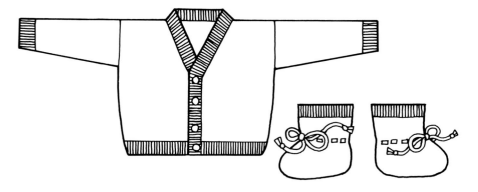

Materials

Small (½oz) balls of Shetland 2 ply wool in 9 contrast colours.

With 2¾mm needles and 1st contrast on colour chart cast on 46 (50:56) sts. Work in K1 P1 rib to row 4 on chart. Change to 3¼mm needles and st st. Work downwards from chart.

1st size only
Work from row 15 to 25 on chart.
2nd and 3rd size
Work from chart from row 1 to 25.
All sizes
With main colour (beige) P1 row.
Next row: K1,* yfwd, K2 tog, rep from* to last stitch, K1.
Next row: P to end.

Shape toe
Next row: K28[32:36] sts, turn, leaving rem sts on holder.
Next row: P10[14:16] sts, turn, leaving rem sts on 2nd holder.
Work 0[2:4] rows in st st.
Working from row 26 to 38, work a single mushroom motif over the centre sts. Dec 1 st at each end of last row.

Foot
With right side of work facing and colour contrast of next patt row, K across 18[18:20] sts from 1st holder, pick up and K8[12:16] sts from side of toe, K across 8[12:14] sts from toe, pick up and K8[12:16] sts from 2nd side of toe, K across 18[18:20] sts from 2nd holder (60[72:86] sts).
Work a further 7 rows in patt from chart.
Next row: Continue in patt, K2 tog, K22[26:32], K2 tog, K8[12:14], K2 tog, K22[26:32], K2 tog.
Next row: Change to main colour, P2 tog, P21[25:31], P2 tog, P6[10:12], P2 tog, P21[25:31], P2 tog.
Next row: K2 tog, K20[24:30], K2 tog, K4[8:10], K2 tog, K20[24:30], K2 tog.
Next row: P2 tog, P19[23:29], P2 tog, P2[6:8], P2 tog, P19[23:29], P2 tog.
1st size only
Cast off.
2nd and 3rd size
K2 tog, K22[28], K2 tog, K4[6], K2 tog, K22[28], K2 tog.
Cast off.

TO MAKE UP
Join back and underfoot seams.
Make a twisted cord from 3 lengths of contrast colour, each 110cm long (see Techniques).
Thread through eyelet holes.

This basic bootee pattern can be adapted to other designs.

Change to 3¼mm needles.
Beg with 9th[1st] row of chart work in patt inc 1 st each end of 3rd and every foll 8th row until there are 50[58] sts.
Cont without shaping until 43rd row of chart.
Cont in main colour until sleeve measures 14[16]cm from beg, ending with a wrong side row. Cast off.

NECKBAND
Join shoulder seams.
With right side facing, 2¾mm needles and main colour (beige) pick up and K74[84] sts up right front, K across 20[24] sts at back neck, pick up and K74[84] sts from left front (168[192] sts).
Work 3 rows K1, P1 rib.
Girl's version
Buttonhole row: Rib 4, (yfwd, P2 tog, rib 8) 3 times, yfwd, P2 tog, rib to end.
Boy's version
Buttonhole row: Rib to last 36 sts, (yfwd, P2 tog, rib 8) 3 times, yfwd, P2 tog, rib 4.

Both versions
Work 2 more rows rib in main colour. Change to 1st contrast (rust) and work 1 row rib. Cast off.

TO MAKE UP
Darn in all ends.
Press pieces lightly on wrong side under a damp cloth.
Sew in sleeves. Join side and sleeve seams.
Sew on buttons to correspond with buttonholes.
With right side facing, 2.50mm crochet hook and 1st contrast, work a row of dc along lower edge on each side of neckband to join up stripe at start of welt with stripe on edge of neckband.

BOOTEES
In 2 different pattern combinations.

Sizes
From birth to 6 months.
Length of foot 9.5[11.5:13.5]cm (3½[4½:5½]in).

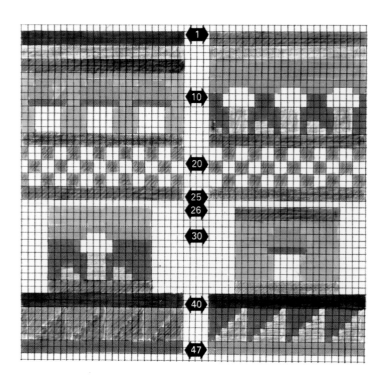

Fruity cardigan & bootees

Pattern repeat 4 sts and 56 rows

Sizes
To fit 40[46]cm (16[18]in) chest.
Length 18[23]cm (7[9]in).
Sleeve seam 14[16]cm (5½[6½]in).

Materials
1 skein of Shetland 2 ply wool in main colour (white).
1 skein each of 8 contrast colours (beige, pink, mauve, bright green, apple green, blue, yellow, rust).
Pair 2¾mm (No 12) needles.
Pair 3¼mm (No 10) needles.
2.50mm (No 12) crochet hook (optional).
4 small buttons.

Tension
30 sts and 34 rows to 10cm (4in) over patt worked on 3¼mm needles.

BACK AND FRONTS (worked in one piece to armholes)
With 2¾mm needles and 1st contrast (beige) cast on 116[132] sts.
Work 1 row K1, P1 rib.
Change to main colour (white) and work 5 more rows in rib.
Change to 3¼mm needles.
Work 1 row K, 1 row P.

1st size only
Beg with the 1st row of chart, work in patt for 34 rows.

2nd size only
Beg with 1st row of chart, work in patt for 38 rows.

Shape neck (both sizes)
Keeping patt correct, work 2 tog, work to last 2 sts, work 2 tog. Work 1 row.

Divide for armholes
Next row: Work 2 tog, patt across 27[35] sts for right front, turn, leaving rem sts on holder.
Keeping armhole edge straight, cont

dec at neck edge every alt row until 18[20] sts rem.
Cont without shaping until 60[72] rows have been worked (rows 4[16] of chart). Cast off.
Rejoin yarn to rem sts and patt across 56[64] sts for back, turn and leave rem sts on holder.

Keeping armhole edges straight work in patt until back measures same as for front shoulder edge.
Cast off 18[20] sts at beg of next 2 rows. Leave rem sts on holder.
Rejoin yarn to sts for left front and complete to match right front reversing all shaping.

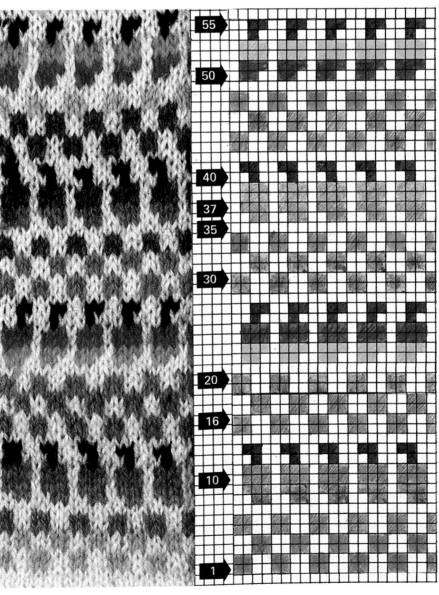

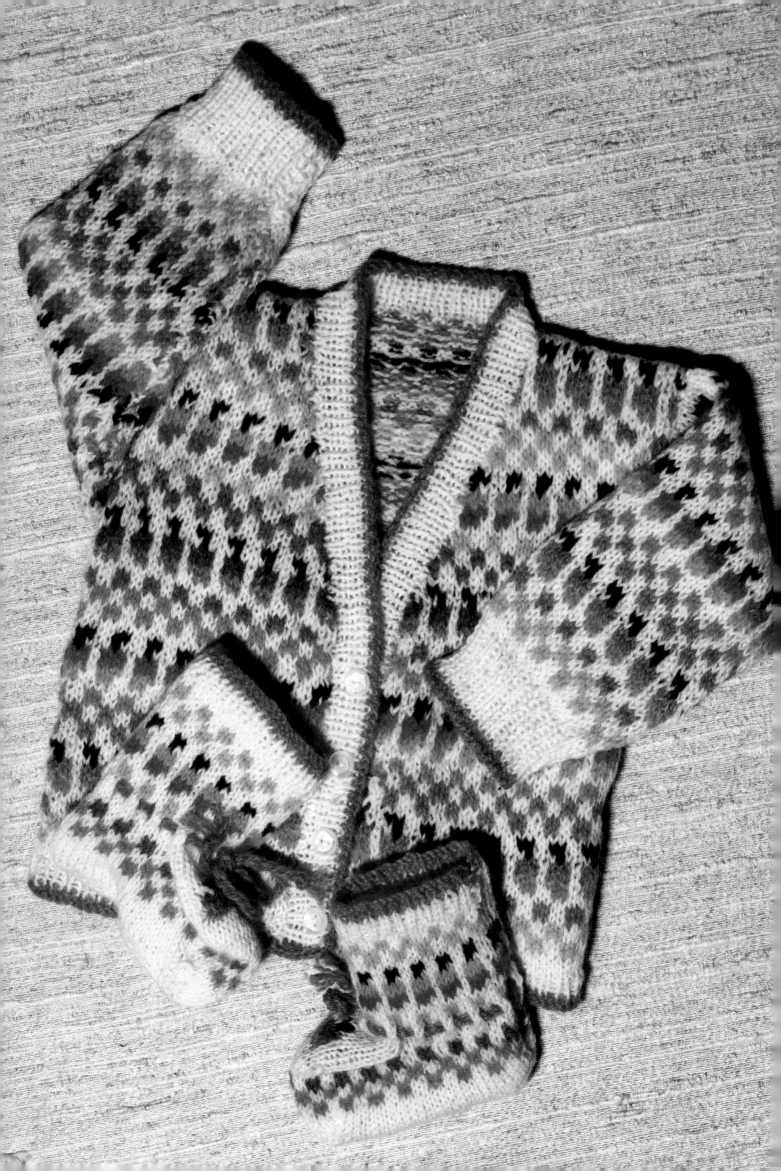

SLEEVES

With 2¾mm needles and 1st contrast (beige) cast on 40[46] sts.
Work 1 row K1, P1 rib.
Change to main colour (white) and work 10 more rows in rib.
Change to 3¼mm needles.
Beg with 1st[1st] row of chart work in patt inc 1 st each end of 3rd and every foll 8th row until there are 50[58] sts.
Cont without shaping until 34th[42nd] row of chart.
With main colour (white) K1 row P1 row. Cast off.

NECKBAND

Join shoulder seams.
With right side facing, 2¾mm needles and main colour pick up and K74[84] sts up right front, K across 20[24] sts at back neck, pick up and K74[84] sts from left front (168[192] sts).
Work 3 rows K1, P1 rib.

Girl's version
Buttonhole row: Rib 4, (yfwd, P2 tog, rib 8) 3 times, yfwd, P2 tog, rib to end.

Boy's version
Buttonhole row: Rib to last 36 sts, (yfwd, P2 tog, rib 8) 3 times, yfwd, P2 tog, rib 4.

Both versions
Work 2 more rows rib in main colour. Change to 1st contrast (beige) and work 1 row rib. Cast off.

TO MAKE UP

Darn in all ends.
Press pieces lightly on wrong side under a damp cloth.
Sew in sleeves. Join side and sleeve seams.
Sew on buttons to correspond with buttonholes.
With right side facing, 2.50mm crochet hook and 1st contrast, work a row of dc along lower edge on each side of neckband to join up stripe at start of welt with stripe on edge of neckband.

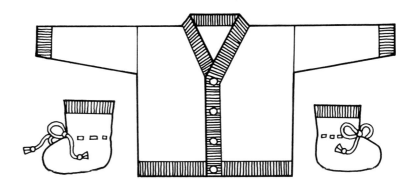

BOOTEES

Sizes
From birth to 6 months.
Length of foot 9.5[11.5:13.5]cm (3½[4½:5½]in).

Materials
Small (½oz) balls of Shetland 2 ply wool in 9 contrast colours.

With 2¾mm needles and 1st contrast (beige) cast on 46[50:56] sts.
Work 1 row in K1 P1 rib.
Change to main colour (white) and work a further 3 rows in rib.
Change to 3¼mm needles. Work 2 rows st st.
Reverse chart so that the fruit hang the right way up.
Beg with row 1 of chart, work down to row 47.
P1 row in main colour (white).
Working with colour now on needles make eyelet holes as follows:
Next row: K1,* yfwd, K2 tog, rep from* to last st, K1.
Next row: P to end.

Shape toe
Next row: K28[32:36], turn, leaving rem sts on holder.
Next row: P10[14:16], turn, leaving rem sts on 2nd holder.
Work 2[4:6] more rows in st st.
Working from row 41 to 36 of chart work two fruit motifs on 7 centre sts.
Beg with a K row work 4 more rows st st, dec 1 st each end of last row. Break yarn.

Foot
With right side of work facing and main colour (white), K across 18[18:20] sts from 1st holder, pick up and K8[12:16] sts from side of toe, K across 8[12:14] sts of toe, pick up and K8[12:16] sts from 2nd side of toe, pick up and K across 18[18:20] sts from 2nd holder (60[72:86] sts).
Work rows 34 to 31 from chart.
Next row: In main colour (white) P1 row.
Next row: K2 tog, K22[26:32], K2 tog, K8[12:14], K2 tog, K22[26:32], K2 tog.
Next row: P2 tog, P21[25:31], P2 tog, P6[10:12], P2 tog, P21[25:31], P2 tog.
Next row: K2 tog, K20[24:30], K2 tog, K4[8:10], K2 tog, K20, K2 tog.
Next row: P2 tog, P19[23:29], P2 tog, P2[6:8], P2 tog, P19[23:29], P2 tog.

1st size only
Cast off.

2nd and 3rd sizes
Next row: K2 tog, K22[28], K2 tog, K4[6], K2 tog, K22[28], K2 tog.
Next row: P2 tog, P21[27], P2 tog, P2[4], P2 tog, P21[27], P2 tog. Cast off.

TO MAKE UP

Join seams.
Make a twisted cord from 3 lengths of contrast colour 110cm long (see Techniques). Thread through eyelet holes.

Butterflies cardigan & bootees

Pattern repeat 6 sts and 38 rows

Sizes
To fit 41[46:51]cm (16[18:20]in) chest.
Length 18[23:28]cm (7[9:11]in).
Sleeve seam 13[17:20]cm (5[6¾:8]in).

Materials
2 skeins of Shetland 2 ply wool in main colour (white).
1 skein of each of 4 contrast colours (blue, beige, pink, yellow).
Pair 2¾mm (No 12) needles.
Pair 3¼mm (No 10) needles.
2.50mm (No 12) crochet hook (optional).
3[4:5] small buttons.

Tension
30 sts and 34 rows to 10cm (4in) over patt worked on 3¼mm needles.

BACK
With 2¾mm needles and 1st contrast (blue) cast on 64[72:82] sts.
Work 1 row K1, P1 rib.
Change to 2nd contrast (beige). Work a further 5[7:9] rows rib.
Change to 3¼mm needles.
All sizes
Beg with a K row work in patt from chart for 5 rows.
1st size only
Beg at row 17 of chart, patt to row 64 on chart. Work 2 rows st st in colour now on needles.
2nd size only
Beg at row 6 of chart, patt to row 73 on chart.
Work 1 row in colour on needles.
3rd size only
Beg at row 6 of chart, patt to row 73, then work rows 36 to 45 incl.
All sizes
Cast off 21[24:26] sts at beg of next 2 rows.
Leave rem 22[24:30] sts on holder for neckband.

LEFT FRONT
With 2¾mm needles and 1st contrast (blue) cast on 32[38:44] sts and work as given for back until 30[40:50] rows of pattern have been worked, ending at armhole edge.

Shape neck
Dec 1 st at neck edge on next and every foll alt row until 21[24:26] sts rem.
Cont without shaping until front measures same as back to shoulder.
Cast off.
Work right front to match left, reversing all shaping.

SLEEVES
With 2¾mm needles and 1st contrast (blue) cast on 40[46:52] sts.
Work 1 row K1, P1 rib.
Change to 2nd contrast (beige).
Work a further 11 rows rib.
Change to 3¼mm needles.
Work 0[2:4] rows st st main colour.
Inc 1 st at each end of 5th and every foll 6th row until there are 48[60:66] sts. Work in patt as follows:
Work rows 1 to 5 from chart.
Beg at row 17[6:36] of chart, cont in patt until 34[48:17] rows have been worked from end of rib.
3rd size only
Still inc every 6th row, work from row 6 of chart until 58 rows have been worked from end of rib.
All sizes
Cast off.

NECKBAND
Join shoulder seams.
With right side of work facing, 2¾mm needles and 2nd contrast (beige) pick up and K56[74:84] sts up right front, K across 22[24:30] sts from holder at back neck, pick up and K56[74:84] sts down left front (134[172:198] st).
Work 3 rows K1, P1 rib.

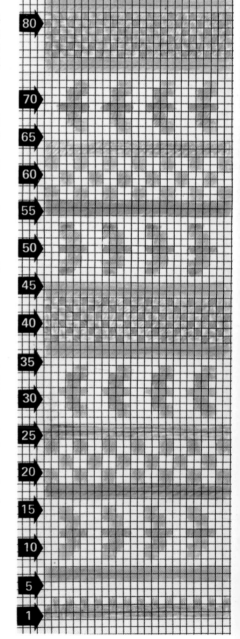

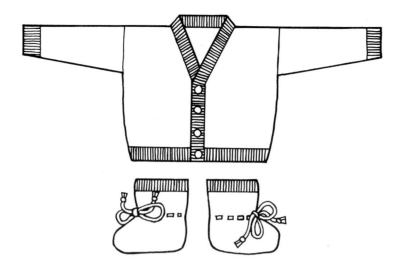

Next row: Rib 4, (yfwd, K2 tog, rib 10) 3[4:5] times, rib to end.
Work 2 more rows in 2nd contrast (beige).
Change to 1st contrast, work 2 rows and cast off.

TO MAKE UP

Sew in sleeve. Join side and sleeve seams.
With right side facing, 2.50mm crochet hook and 1st contrast work a few dc along lower edge of neckband on each side, linking cast-on edge of neckband.
Sew on buttons.

BOOTEES

Sizes

From birth to 6 months.
Length of foot 9.5[11.5:13.5]cm (3½[4½:5½]in).

Materials

Small (½oz) balls of Shetland 2 ply wool in 5 contrast colours.

With 2¾mm needles and 1st contrast (blue) cast on 46[50:56] sts.
Work 1 row K1, P1 rib.
Change to 2nd contrast (beige) and work a further 5 rows rib.
Change to 3¼mm needles.
Work 2 rows st st in main colour (white).
Beg with row 16 of chart work 12 rows in patt.
Working in colour now on needles work eyelet holes as follows:
Next row: K1, *yfwd, K2 tog, rep from * to last st, K1.
Next row: P to end.

Shape toe

Next row: K28[32:36], turn, leaving rem sts on holder.

Next row: P10[14:16], turn, leaving rem st on 2nd holder.
Work 2[4:6] more rows st st.
Working from row 28 to 34 of chart work a single butterfly motif over the centre 4 sts.
Beg with a P row work 3 more rows st st, dec 1 st at each end of last row.
Break yarn.

Foot

With right side of work facing and beg from row 36 of chart, knit across 18[18:20] sts from first holder, pick up and K8[12:16] sts from side of toe, K across 8[12:14] sts of toe, pick up and K8[12:16] sts from 2nd side of toe, K across 18[18:20] sts from 2nd holder (60[72:86] sts).
Work a further 7 rows from chart.
Next row: In next colour K2 tog, K22[26:32], K2 tog, K8[12:14], K2 tog, K22[26:32], K2 tog.
Next row: P2 tog, P21[25:31], P2 tog, P6[10:12], P2 tog, P21[25:31], P2 tog.
Next row: Change to main colour (white), K2 tog, K20[24:30], K2 tog, K4[8:10], K2 tog, K20, K2 tog.
Next row: P2 tog, P19[23:29], P2 tog, P2[6:8], P2 tog, P19[23:29], P2 tog.
1st size only
Next row: Cast off.
2nd and 3rd sizes
Next row: K2 tog, K22[28], K2 tog, K4[6], K2 tog, K22[28], K2 tog.
Next row: P2 tog, P21[27], P2 tog, P2[4], P2 tog, P21[27], P2 tog.
Next row: Cast off.

TO MAKE UP

Join back and under-foot seam.
Make a twisted cord from 3 lengths of 1st contrast each 110cm long (see Techniques).
Thread through eyelet holes.

Basil Pots & Bees jumpers

Pattern repeat 8, 7, 6 sts and 70 rows

Size
To fit 51cm (20in) chest.
Length 25.5cm (10in).
Sleeve length 19cm (7½in).

Materials
1 skein of Shetland 2 ply wool in main colour (beige or navy).
1 skein each of 7 contrast colours.
(1st combination: olive green, brown, pink, white, rust, grey-green, blue, green; 2nd combination: blue, yellow, green, rust, olive green, white, pale green).
Pair 2¾mm (No 12) needles.
Pair 3¼mm (No 10) needles.
One 2.50mm (No 12) crochet hook (optional).
4 buttons.

Tension
30 sts and 34 rows to 10cm (4in) over patt worked on 3¼mm needles.

BACK
With 2¾mm needles and 1st contrast colour (rust, blue) cast on 72 sts.
Work 1 row K1, P1 rib.
Change to 2nd contrast (olive green, yellow).
Work 2 rows K1, P1 rib.
Change to main colour (beige, navy) and cont in K1, P1 rib for 3cm.
Change to 3¼mm needles.
Work in patt from chart for 70 rows.
Work 4 more rows in main colour (beige or navy).

Shape shoulder
Cast off 18 sts at beg of next row for right shoulder.
Next row: Work in K1, P1 rib across 1st 18 sts, turn, leaving rem 36 sts on holder for back neck.
Work 2 more rows in K1, P1 rib. Cast off.

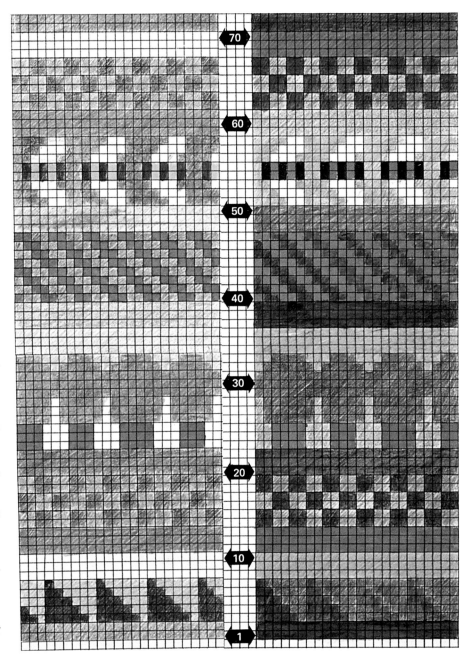

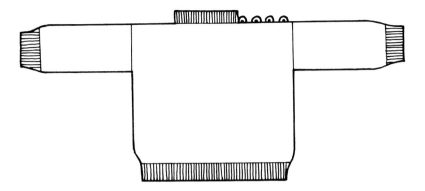

FRONT

Work as for back to row 70 on chart.

Shape neck

With main colour (beige, navy), work across 22 sts, turn and leave rem sts on holder.
Dec st at neck edge on next 4 rows.
Change to 2¾mm needles and work 2 rows in K1, P1 rib. Cast off.
Leaving the 28 centre sts on holder, rejoin yarn and patt to end of row.
Dec 1 st at neck edge of next 4 rows. Cast off.

SLEEVES

With 2¾mm needles and 1st contrast colour (rust, blue) cast on 46 sts.
Work in rib as for back for 5cm.
Change to 3¼mm needles.
Work from row 1 to 47 on patt chart, inc 1 st each end of 3rd row and every foll 6th row until there are 76 sts. Cast off.

NECKBAND

Join right shoulder seam.
With right side facing and 2¾mm needles and main colour (beige, navy) pick up and K4 sts down right side of front neck, K across 28 sts on holder, pick up and K4 sts up left side of neck, K across 36 sts on holder at back neck (72) sts.
Work 6 rows K1, P1 rib.
Change to 2nd contrast colour (olive green, yellow) and work 2 rows in rib.
Change to 1st contrast (rust, blue). Cast off.

TO MAKE UP

Darn in all ends. Press pieces lightly on wrong side under a damp cloth.
Join left shoulder for about 1cm. Sew in sleeves. Join side and sleeve seams. Sew on 4 buttons to left shoulder on back. Crochet (or work by hand) 4 button loops to correspond with buttons.

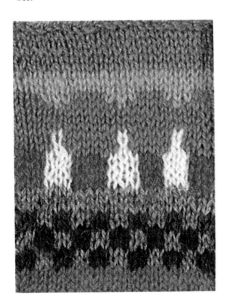

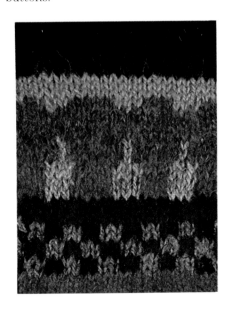

Berries & Bees baby's cap, mitts and bootees

Pattern repeat 8 sts and 30 rows for bumble bees, 6 sts and 31 rows for berries

Sizes
To fit 0-3[3-6] months.
Measurement round head 40[44]cm (16[17]in).

Materials (cap and mitts)
1 skein of Shetland 2 ply wool in each of 6 colours (greeny-blue, yellow, beige, navy, orange, white for bumble bees; red, navy, yellow, green, beige, blue for berries).
Pair 2¾mm (No 12) needles.
Pair 3¼mm (No 10) needles.
2.50mm (No 12) crochet hook.

Tension
30 sts and 34 rows to 10cm (4in) over patt worked on 3¼mm needles.

CAP
With 2¾mm needles and first contrast cast on 120[130] sts.
Work 1 row in K1, P1 rib.
Bumble bees only
Change to 2nd contrast and work 2 rows in rib, then in 3rd contrast work 3 rows rib.
Berries only
Change to 3rd contrast and cont in rib for 5 rows.
Bumble bees and berries
Change to 3¼mm needles.
Beg with a K row, work in patt from chart for 26[30] rows, ending with a wrong side row.

Shape crown
1st row: (K2 tog, K8) 12[13] times.
2nd row: P to end.
3rd row: (K2 tog, K7) 12[13] times.
4th row: P to end.
5th row: (K2 tog, K6) 12[13] times.
6th row: P to end.
Cont to dec in this way, working 1 st less between each dec until 48[49] sts

rem, ending with a wrong side row.
Next row: K0[1], (K2 tog) 24 times.
Break off yarn, thread through rem sts on needle, draw up tightly and fasten off securely.

Ear flaps
With right side of lower edge facing, 3¼mm needles and 3rd contrast for bumble bees or 2nd contrast for berries, miss first 16[18] sts, pick up and K next 14[16] sts.
Beg with a P row, work 5 rows st st.
Dec 1 st each end of every row until 6 sts rem.
Cast off.
Miss the next 60[62] sts, rejoin yarn and work 2nd ear flap to match first.

TO MAKE UP
Join centre back seam.
With right side facing, 2.50mm crochet hook and 2nd contrast for bumble bees or 4th contrast colour for berries, work 1 row of dc round edge of flap, fasten off.
With right side facing join in 1st contrast and work 1dc into each dc of previous row.
Repeat on 2nd ear flap.
Make 2 lengths of twisted cord (see Techniques) or crocheted ch 35cm long in same colour as first row of dc. Stitch to centre of ear flap.
Make tassels (see Techniques) in the 1st contrast and stitch to the end of each cord.
Make a pompon (see Techniques) in the same colour as ear flap and stitch to top of hat.

MITTS
With 2¾mm needles and 1st contrast cast on 42[48] sts.
Work 1 row K1, P1 rib.
Bumble bees only
Change to 2nd contrast and work 2 rows in rib, then in 3rd contrast work 11 rows rib.

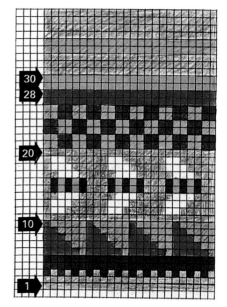

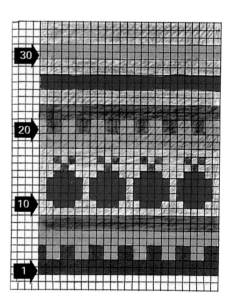

Berries only
Change to 3rd contrast and cont in rib for 13 rows.
Bumble bees and berries
Eyelet hole row: K1, *yfwd, K2 tog, rep from * to last st, K1.

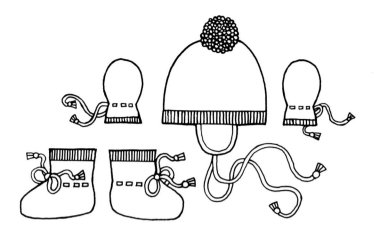

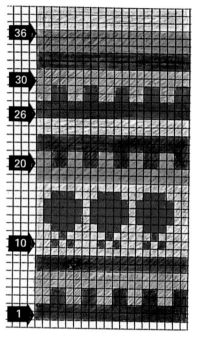

Change to 3¼mm needles.
Next row: P to end.
Beg with a K row, work in patt from chart for 26 rows starting at row 1 of chart (start at row 6 for 1st size only bumble bee).
Cont in 1 colour only dec as foll:
Next row: *K2 tog, K2, rep from * to end.
Next row: *P2 tog, P1, rep from * to end.

TO MAKE UP
Join side seams.
Make 2 lengths of twisted cord (see Techniques) or crocheted ch 28cm long in same colour as for hat.
Thread through eyelet holes at wrist.
Make 4 tassels in contrast colour to cap and stitch to each end of ties (see Techniques).

BOOTEES

Note
As the bootees are worked from top to toe, the motifs appear to be upside down on the charts.

Sizes
From birth to 6 months.
Length of foot 9.5[11.5:13.5]cm (3½[4½:5½]in).

Materials
Oddments of Shetland 2 ply wool in 6 contrast colours (greeny-blue, yellow, beige, navy, orange, white for bumble bees; red, navy, yellow, green, beige, blue for berries).
Pair 2¾mm (No 12) needles.
Pair 3¼mm (No 10) needles.

Tension
30 sts and 34 rows to 10cm (4in) over patt worked on 3¼mm needles.

Bumble bees only
With 2¾mm needles and 1st contrast (greeny-blue) cast on 46[50:56] sts.

Work 1 row K1, P1 rib.
Change to 2nd contrast (yellow) and work a further 2 rows rib.
Change to main colour (beige) and work 1 row rib.
Change to 3¼mm needles and work from chart from row 1 to 19. For 1st size, work row 1 to 9 only.
Berries only
With 2¾mm needles and 1st contrast (red) cast on 46[50:56] sts.
Work 1 row K1, P1 rib.
Change to 2nd contrast (navy) and work a further 2 rows rib.
Change to 3¼mm needles and work from chart from row 1 to 23.
For 1st size work row 9 to 23 only.
Bumble bees and berries
Change to beige yarn. P 1 row.
Next row: Work eyelet holes as follows: K1, *yfwd, K2 tog, rep from * to last st, K1.
Next row: P to end.

Shape toe
Next row: K28[32:36], turn leaving rem sts on holder.
Next row: P10[14:16], turn leaving rem sts on 2nd holder.
Bumble bees only
Work 1[3:5] more rows st st.
Working from row 9 to 16, work a single bee motif over centre 5 sts.
Berries only
Work 2[4:6] more rows st st.
Working from row 10 to 16 of chart, work a single berry motif over centre 5 sts.
Work 3 more rows st st. Dec 1 st each end of last row.
Break yarn.

Foot
Bumble bees and berries
With right side of work facing and beg from row 20 of chart for bumble bees and row 26 for berries, K across 18[18:20] sts from 1st holder, pick up and K8[12:16] sts from side of toe, K across 8[12:14] sts of toe, pick up and

K 8[12:16] sts from 2nd side of toe, K across 18[18:20] sts from 2nd holder (60[72:86] sts).
Work a further 7 rows from chart.
In next colour on chart, K2 tog, K22[26:32], K2 tog, K8[12:14], K2 tog, K22[26:32], K2 tog.
Next row: P2 tog, P21[25:31], P2 tog, P6[10:12], P2 tog, P21[25:31], P2 tog.
Next row: K2 tog, K20[24:30], K2 tog, K4[8:10], K2 tog, K20[24:30], K2 tog.
Next row: P2 tog, P19[23:29], P2 tog, P2[6:8], P2 tog, P19[23:29], P2 tog.
1st size only
Next row: Cast off.
2nd and 3rd sizes
Next row: K2 tog, K22[28], K2 tog, K4[6], K2 tog, K22[28], K2 tog.
Cast off.

TO MAKE UP
Join back and underfoot seam.
Make a twisted cord from 3 lengths of contrast colour each 110cm long (see Techniques).
Thread through eyelet holes.

Comets slipper socks

Child's slipper socks in 2 sizes, made from double knitting wool and tapestry wool of the same thickness. A circular needle is used to give flexibility when working round the toe. The sock is worked flat, knitting to and fro in the usual way.

This pattern can be adapted to many different designs. The main part could be worked in a single colour with a few contrasting stripes, and any of the other motifs elsewhere in the book could be worked on the foot.

Pattern repeat: Main design, 12 and 8 sts and 44 rows
Comet Motif, 11 sts and 11 rows

Measurements
Length of foot 16.5[18]cm (6½[7]in).
Leg seam 19cm (7½in).

Materials
28g (1oz) of double knitting wool in main colour (navy).
3 skeins (15yd each) of tapestry wool in 3 contrast colours (orange, green and yellow).
5 skeins of tapestry wool (or 1oz double knitting) in 4th contrast (blue).
4 skeins of tapestry wool in 5th contrast (cream).
2 skeins of tapestry wool in 6th contrast (red).
Size 3mm (No 11) circular needle 60cm long.
25 × 25cm (10 × 10in) suede, imitation suede or firm material.
25 × 25cm (10 × 10in) cardboard.

Tension
30 sts and 34 rows to 10cm (4in) over patt worked on 3mm needles.

LEG
With main colour (navy) and 3mm needle, cast on 60 sts.
K2, P2 rib for 4 rows.

Change to 1st contrast (orange), work 3 rows in rib.
Change to 2nd contrast (green), work 3 rows in rib.
Change to 3rd contrast (yellow), work 3 rows in rib.
Change to 4th contrast (blue), work 4cm (1½in) in rib.
Change to main colour (navy) and work in st st from chart starting at row 1. Cont to row 32.
Row 33: Slip the 1st and last 22 sts onto 2 separate holders (yarn or stitch holders).
Working on the 16 centre sts, start with a K row and 4th contrast (blue). Work 6[10] rows in st st.
Work a single comet motif over centre st as given on chart.

FOOT
With right side of work facing and beg from row 33 of chart, K across 22 sts on 1st holder, pick up and K 18[22] sts from side of toe, K across 16 sts of toe, pick up and K 18[22] sts from 2nd side of toe, K across 22 sts on 2nd holder (96[104] sts).
Work to row 44 of chart.
Cast off.

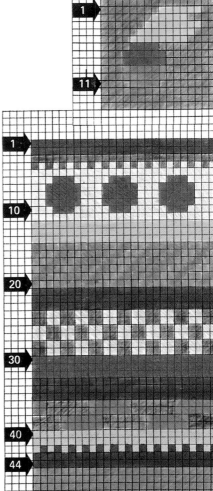

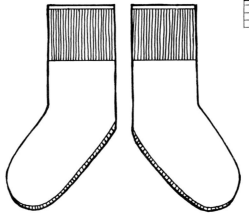

SOLES

Inner knitted sole

With main colour (navy), cast on 8 sts.

Work in st st inc at beg of every row until there are 18 sts.

Work straight for 6.5cm (2½in).

Dec at each end of every 4th row until there are 12 sts.

Work straight until work measures 16[17.5]cm (6¼[6¾]in).

Dec 1 st at beg and end of each row until there are 4 sts left.

Cast off.

Iron under damp cloth.

Outer sole

Trace pattern of sole on to cardboard. Cut 2.

Suede only:

Lay cardboard soles on top of suede.

Pencil round edge.

Cut on pencil line.

Imitation suede and material:

Lay cardboard soles on top of material.

Pencil round edge.

Cut out, leaving a small 3mm (⅛in) seam allowance.

TO MAKE UP

Sew up leg seams.

With smooth side of knitted sole facing inwards, tack to sock.

Overstitch tog at edge of work.

Turn right side out.

Place cardboard sole inside sock.

Tie a tape firmly round ankle to keep cardboard in place.

Tack in place, oversew round edge (making a small turning all round for imitation suede and material soles only).

Finish off with buttonhole st.

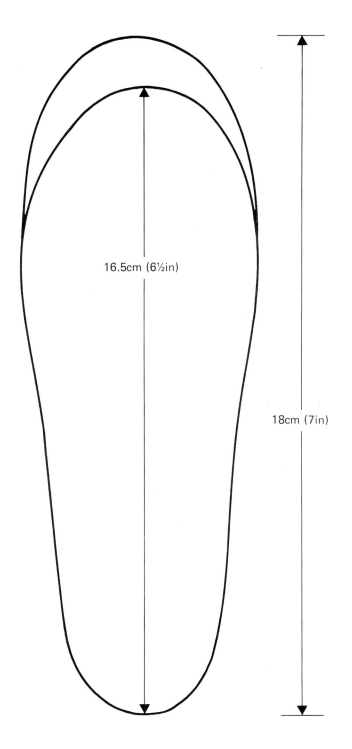

16.5cm (6½in)

18cm (7in)

Oranges & Lemons jumper

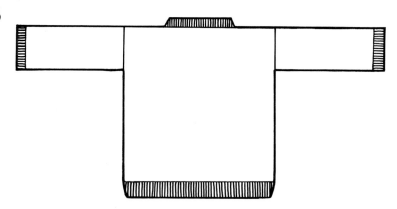

Pattern repeat 6 sts and 78 rows

Sizes

To fit 51[61:71]cm (20[24:28]in) chest.
Length 31.5[34.5:35.5]cm (12½ [13½:14]in).
Sleeve seam 22[25.5:30]cm (8¾[10: 11¾]in).

Materials

3 skeins of Shetland 2 ply wool in main colour (dusty yellow).
1 skein each of 6 contrast colours (brown, greeny-blue, dark green, bright green, bright yellow, orange).
Pair 2¾mm (No 12) needles.
Pair 3¼mm (No 10) needles.

Tension

30 sts and 34 rows to 10cm (4in) over patt worked on 3¼mm needles.

BACK

With 2¾mm needles and main colour (dusty yellow) cast on 84[96:108] sts.
Work in K1, P1 rib for 6 rows.
Change to 3¼mm needles.
Beg with a K row work 4 rows st st.
Starting on the 13th[1st:1st] row of chart, work 108[116:120] rows in patt.
Cast off 15[16:20] sts at beg of next 2 rows.
Change to 2¾mm needles.
Work 6 rows in K1, P1 rib in main colour (dusty yellow).
Cast off.

FRONT

Work as given for back.

SLEEVES

With 2¾mm needles and main colour (dusty yellow) cast on 76[76:82] sts.
Work in K1, P1 rib for 6 rows.
Change to 3¼mm needles.
Beg with a K row 4 rows in st st.
Starting with 13th[1st:1st] row from chart, work 63[76:90] rows in patt.
Cast off.

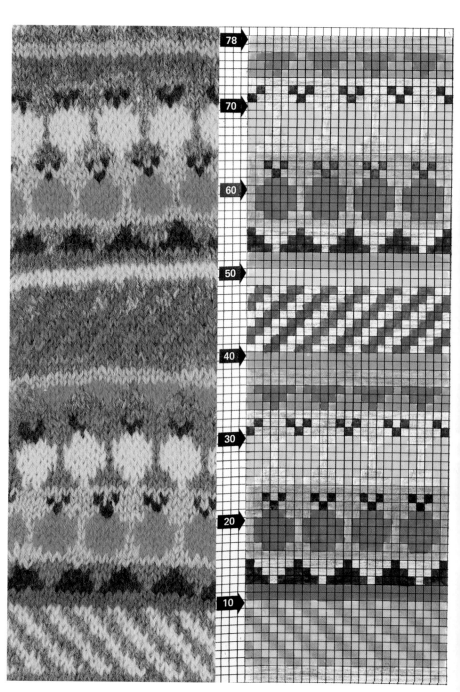

TO MAKE UP

Join shoulder seams. Sew in sleeves.
Join side and sleeve seams.
Fold side edges of front neck ribbing diagonally over to back neck and slip stitch along back neckline.
Stitch back neck ribbing in the same way to inside front neck.

Bumble Bees jumper

Pattern repeat 8 sts and 76 rows

Sizes
To fit 56[61]cm (22[24]in) chest.
Length 28[34]cm (11[13½]in).
Sleeve seam 18[26]cm (7[10½]in).

Materials
2 skeins of Shetland 2 ply wool in main colour (beige).
1 skein each of 7 contrast colours (turquoise, gold, white, orange, dark green, rust, navy).
Pair 2¾mm (No 12) needles.
Pair 3¼mm (No 10) needles.
2.50mm crochet hook (optional).
4 small buttons.

Tension
30 sts and 34 rows to 10cm (4in) over patt worked on 3¼mm needles.

BACK
With 2¾mm needles and 1st colour (turquoise) cast on 79[89] sts.
Change to 2nd colour (gold).
Next row: K1, *P1, K1, rep from * to end.
Change to main colour (beige) and cont in K1, P1 rib for 3cm.
Pick up 11[10] sts on last rib row (90[99] sts).
Change to 3¼mm needles. Work in patt from chart for 80[98] rows (to row 5 and 22 on chart).

1st size only
Work 2 more rows in st st with 1st contrast (turquoise).

Right shoulder
Cast off 23[27] sts at beg of next row.
Leave centre sts on holder.

Left shoulder
Work in K1, P1 rib across first 23[27] sts, turn, leaving rem 45 sts for back neck.
Work 2 more rows in K1, P1 rib. Cast off.

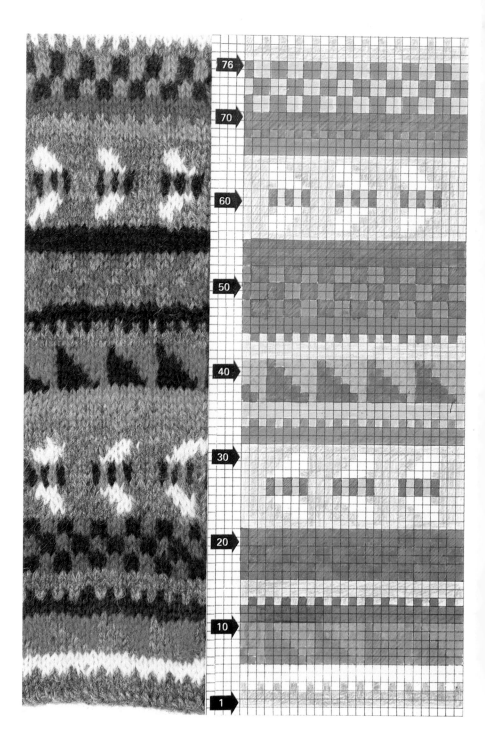

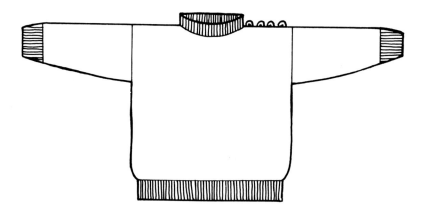

FRONT

Work as for back until 76[88] rows have been worked from chart.

Shape neck

Work across 31[35] sts, turn and leave rem sts on holder.
Dec 1 st at neck edge on next 8 rows.
Change to 2¾mm needles and work 2 rows in K1, P1 rib. Cast off.
Leave first 28[29] of rem sts on holder, rejoin yarn and patt to end of row (31[35] sts).
Dec 1 st at neck edge on next 8 rows. Cast off.

SLEEVES

With 2¾mm needles and 1st colour (turquoise) cast on 46[50] sts.
Change to 2nd colour (gold).

Work 1 row in K1, P1 rib. Change to main colour (beige).
Work rib as given for back for 5cm.
Change to 3¼mm needles.

1st size only

Working in patt from chart, inc 1 st each end of 3rd and every foll 6th row until there are 76 sts.

2nd size only

Working the last 23 rows from the chart first starting at top row of bumble bees (row 56) then starting again from row 6, inc 1 st each end of 3rd and every foll 6th row until there are 90 sts.

Both sizes

Cont without shaping until 54[72] rows of patt have been worked. Cast off.

BUTTONBAND

With wrong side of back facing and 2¾mm needles, rejoin yarn to sts for left shoulder.
Work in K1, P1 rib across the first 23[27] sts, turn leaving rem 45 sts for back neck.
Work 2 more rows in rib. Cast off.

NECKBAND

Join right shoulder seam.
With right side facing and 2¾mm needles and main colour (beige) pick up and K15 sts down right side of front neck, K across 28[29] sts on holder, pick up and K15 sts up left side of neck, K across 44[45] sts on holder at back neck (102[104] sts).
Work 6 rows K1, P1 rib.
Change to 2nd colour (gold) and work 2 rows rib.
Change to 1st colour (turquoise) and cast off.

TO MAKE UP

Darn in all ends. Press pieces lightly on wrong side under a damp cloth. Join left shoulder for about 1cm. Sew in sleeves. Join side and sleeve seams. Sew on 4 buttons to left shoulder on back. Crochet (or work by hand) 4 button loops to correspond with buttons.

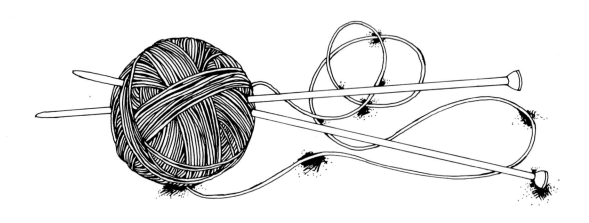

Mushrooms cap & scarf

Pattern repeat 8 sts and 66 rows

This pattern is open to all sorts of variations. The cap could be plain except for a band of motifs worked after the ribbing with the same band repeated on the scarf with other contrasting stripes of colour. The designs for borders on page 116 are very suitable.

Sizes
Cap: 40[48]cm (16[19]in) round head. 17[21]cm (7[8]in) deep.
Scarf: 17cm (6¾in) wide. 140cm (55in) long with 10cm (4in) fringe at each end.

Materials
for cap and scarf:
8 skeins of Shetland 2 ply wool in main colour (yellow).
1 skein each of 6 contrast colours (grey-blue, rust, navy, dark green, olive green, white).
Pair 2¾mm (No 12) needles.
Pair 3¼mm (No 10) needles.
for cap only:
1 skein each of Shetland 2 ply wool in 6 contrast colours.
Pair 2¾mm (No 12) needles.
Pair 3¼mm (No 10) needles.

Tension
30 sts and 34 rows to 10cm (4in) over patt worked on 3¼mm needles.

CAP
With 2¾mm needles and 1st contrast (grey-blue) cast on 130[146] sts and work 2 rows in K1, P1 rib.
Change to 2nd contrast (rust) and work 2 rows in K1, P1 rib.
Change to 3rd contrast (navy) and work 6 rows in K1, P1 rib.
Large size only
Inc 1 st each end of last row.
Both sizes
Change to 3¼mm needles. Beg at row 1 of patt on chart, work 30 rows.

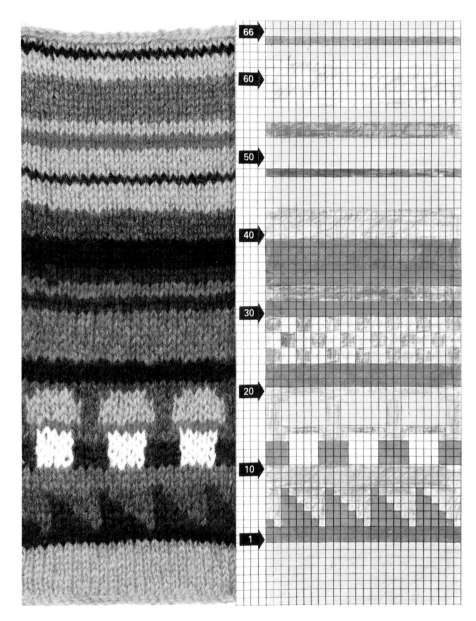

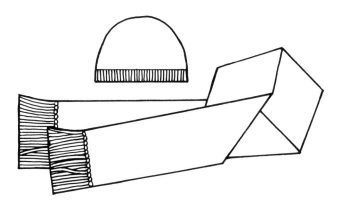

Decrease for crown
Small size only
Cont to follow patt chart.

1st row: (K2 tog, K9), rep to end.

All alt rows P.

3rd row: (K2 tog, K8), rep to end.

Cont in this way until last row is completed which is K2 tog all the way along.

Thread the yarn on needles through these sts and pull through. Use this length of yarn for sewing up.

Large size only
On 1st dec row (31 on patt graph) K3 tog, *K16, K2 tog, rep from * to last 2 sts, K2 tog.

All alt rows P.

3rd row: (K3 tog, K15) twice, (K2 tog, K15) 5 times, K3 tog, K15.

Cont to dec by K2 tog until last row is completed, which is K2 tog all the way along.

Finish as for small size.

SCARF
With 3¼mm needles and main colour (yellow) cast on 117 sts.

Work 8 rows in st st.

Work from graph and after 66th row has been completed, work in main colour for 90cm (35in).

Work from graph, remembering to start from the 66th row and work down to row 1.

Work 8 rows in st st. Cast off.

Fold in half lengthwise and sew up along long edge.

TO MAKE TASSELS
Cut lengths of wool 34cm long and use 4 at a time. Using a large crochet hook, thread 4 strands of wool through the end of the scarf and knot, so that 8 strands hang down. Repeat all along both ends of scarf. When all tassels have been knotted, trim to 10cm in length along bottom with a large pair of sharp scissors.

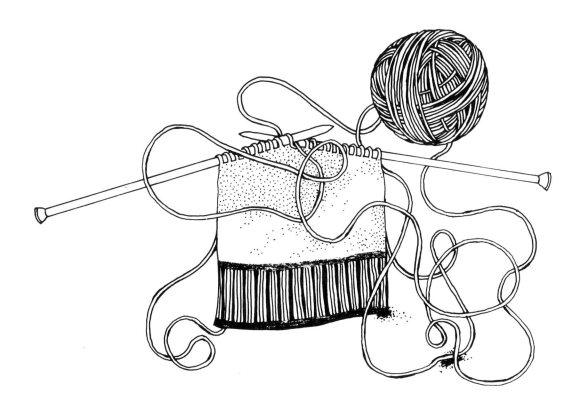

Balloons jumper

Pattern repeat 6 sts and 11 rows

Sizes
To fit 51[61:71]cm (20[24:28]in) chest.
Length 36[39:42]cm (14[15:16½]in).
Sleeve seam 26[29:31]cm (10[11: 12]in).

Materials
1st and 2nd size:
3 skeins Shetland 2 ply wool in main colour (blue).
3rd size:
4 skeins in main colour (blue).
All sizes:
2 skeins of 1st contrast colour (pink).
1 skein each of 3 contrast colours (yellow, orange, green-blue).
Pair 2¾mm (No 12) needles.
Pair 3¼mm (No 10) needles.

Tension
30 sts and 34 rows to 10cm (4in) over patt worked on 3¼mm needles.

BACK
With 2¾mm needles and main colour (blue) cast on 90[98:106] sts.
Work in K1, P1 rib for 6 rows.
Change to 3¼mm needles.
Beg with a K row work 4 rows in st st.
Starting with 1st row of chart, work 110[123:133] rows in patt.
Cast off 15[20:20] sts at beg of next 2 rows.
Change to 2¾mm needles.
Work 6 rows in K1, P1 rib in main colour (blue) on centre 58[60:66] sts.

FRONT
Work as for back.

SLEEVES
With 2¾mm needles and main colour (blue) cast on 74[82:82] sts.
Work in K1, P1 rib for 6 rows.
Change to 3¼mm needles.
Beg with a K row work 4 rows in st st.

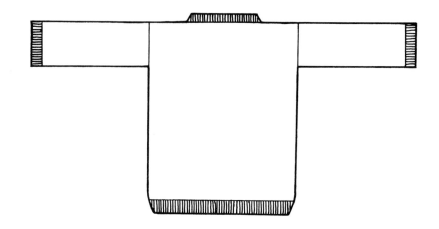

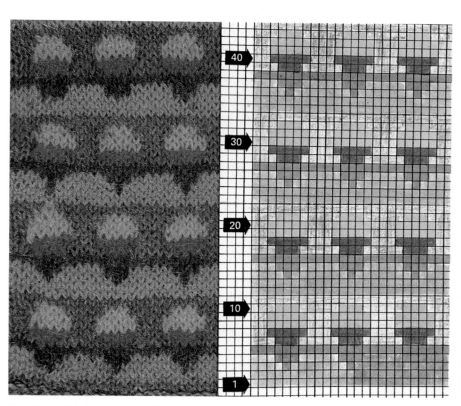

Starting with 1st row of chart, work 77[88:99] rows in patt.
Cast off.

TO MAKE UP
Join shoulder seams. Sew in sleeves.

Join side and sleeve seams.
Fold side edges of front neck ribbing diagonally over to back neck and slip stitch along back neckline.
Stitch back neck ribbing to inside of front neck in the same way.

Wavelets V neck pullover

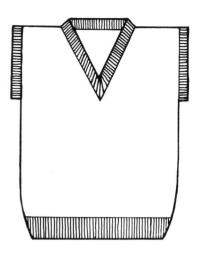

Pattern repeat 6 sts and 14 rows

Sizes
To fit 51[61:71]cm (20[24:28]in) chest.
Length from shoulder to waist 40[41:42]cm (15½[16:16½]in).

Materials
2 skeins of Shetland 2 ply wool in main colour (green).
1 skein each of 3 contrast colours (turquoise, yellow, white).
Pair 2¾mm (No 12) needles.
Pair 3¼mm (No 10) needles.

Tension
30 sts and 34 rows over patt worked on 3¼mm needles.

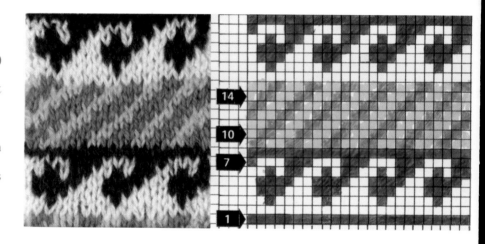

BACK
With 2¾mm needles and 1st contrast (turquoise) cast on 78[90:102] sts.
Work in K1, P1 rib for 2 rows.
Change to main colour (green). Work in rib for 5cm (2in).
Change to 3¼mm needles.
1st and 2nd size only
K row starting at row 7[7] on chart, increase 15 sts evenly along this row (93[105]).
3rd size only
K in colour on needle to end, increasing 15 sts evenly along this row (117 sts).
All sizes
Next row: P starting at row 1 on chart.*
Continue for 55[55:63] rows. Put marker thread at each end of row.
Continue in patt until 106[110:123] rows have been worked (row 8[11:3] of chart).
Cast off 8[10:11] sts at beg of next 2 rows and 9[11:12] at beg of next 4 rows.
Leave centre 43[43:47] sts on holder.

Left front
Work as for back to *
Work from patt on chart for 55[55:63] rows. Put a marker thread at each end of this row.
Keeping armhole edge straight K2 tog at end of every K row until 26[32:36] sts remain.
Continue straight until 108[110:122] rows have been worked (row 8[11:3] of patt on chart).
Next row: Cast off 8[10:11] sts, work to end.
Next row: P.
Next row: Cast off 9[11:12] sts, work to end.
Next row: P.
Next row: Cast off 9[11:12] sts, work to end.
Next row: Cast off.

Right front
Place centre st on safety pin.
Work to match left front reversing all shapings.

NECKBAND
Join right shoulder seam.

With size 2¾mm needles and main colour (green) pick up and K42[47:53] sts from left front, 1 st from safety pin, 42[47:53] sts from right front and 43[43:48] sts from holder (back neck) (128[138:155]).
Work 4 rows in K1, P1 rib, dec 1st each side of centre front st on every row. Change to 1st contrast (turquoise). Work 2 rows in K1, P1 rib, dec 1 st each side of centre front st on every row. Cast off loosely in rib.

ARMBANDS
Join left shoulder seam. Work both armbands alike.
With size 2¾mm needles and main colour (green) pick up 82[90:102] sts between markers.
Work 6 rows in K1, P1 rib.
Change to 1st contrast (turquoise). work 2 rows in K1, P1 rib. Cast off loosely in rib.

TO MAKE UP
Press carefully with damp cloth. Join side seams taking care to match pattern.

Jellyfish V neck pullover

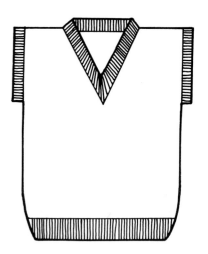

Pattern repeat 10, 12 sts and 48 rows; 1 extra stitch is added at beg of chart so that fish join happily at seam edge

Sizes
To fit 51[61:71]cm (20[24:28]in) chest.
Length from shoulder to waist 40[41:42]cm (15¾[16:16]in).

Materials
2 skeins of Shetland 2 ply wool in main colour (beige).
1 skein each of 6 contrast colours (blue, terracotta, green, mauve, mustard, red).
Pair 2¾mm (No 12) needles.
Pair 3¼mm (No 10) needles.

Tension
30 sts and 34 rows to 10cm (4in) over patt worked on 3¼mm needles.

BACK
With 2¾mm needles and main colour (beige) cast on 82[94:105] sts.
Work for 5cm (2in) in K1, P1 rib.
Change to 3¼mm needles and work from patt chart starting at row 8[8:1] and K.
Increase 16 sts evenly along this row (98[110:122] sts).*
Continue working from patt, remembering to add 1 st at beg of row.
Place marker thread at each end of rows 59 & 60[59 & 60:65 & 66].
Continue to work in patt until 110[114:124] rows have been worked.
Cast off 9[11:13] sts at beg of next 6 rows.
Leave centre 43[43:47] sts on holder.

FRONT
Work as for back to *
Work from patt on chart ending with rows 60[60:66] placing markers as for back.
Left front
Work 48[54:60] sts. Turn.
Leave rem sts on holder.

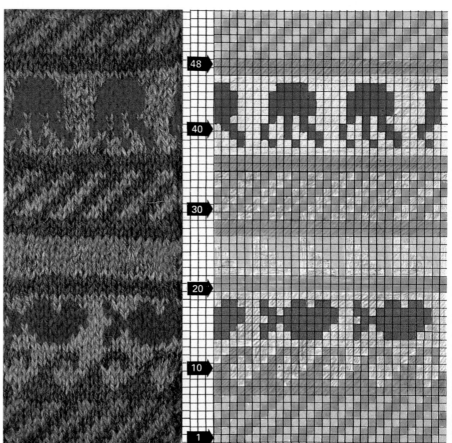

Keeping armhole edge straight K2 tog at end of every K row until 27[33:39] sts remain.
Continue straight until 110[116:124] rows have been worked (rows 24[28:32] on patt chart).
Cast off 9[11:13] sts. Work to end.
Next row: P.
Repeat these 2 rows twice more.
Cast off.
Right front
Place centre st on safety pin.
Work to last 2 sts. K2 tog (48[54:60] sts).
Work right front to match the left, reversing all shapings.

NECKBAND
Join right shoulder seam.
With 2¾mm needles and main colour (beige) pick up and K45[49:53] sts from left front, 1 st from safety pin, K45[49:53] sts from right front and 43[43:47] sts from holder (134[142:154] sts).
Work 8 rows in K1, P1 rib, dec 1 st each side of centre front st on every row. Cast off loosely in rib.

ARMBANDS
Join left shoulder seam and work both armbands alike.
With 2¾mm needles and main colour (beige) pick up 108[112:116] sts between markers.
Work 8 rows in K1, P1 rib. Cast off in rib.

TO MAKE UP
Press carefully. Join side seams.

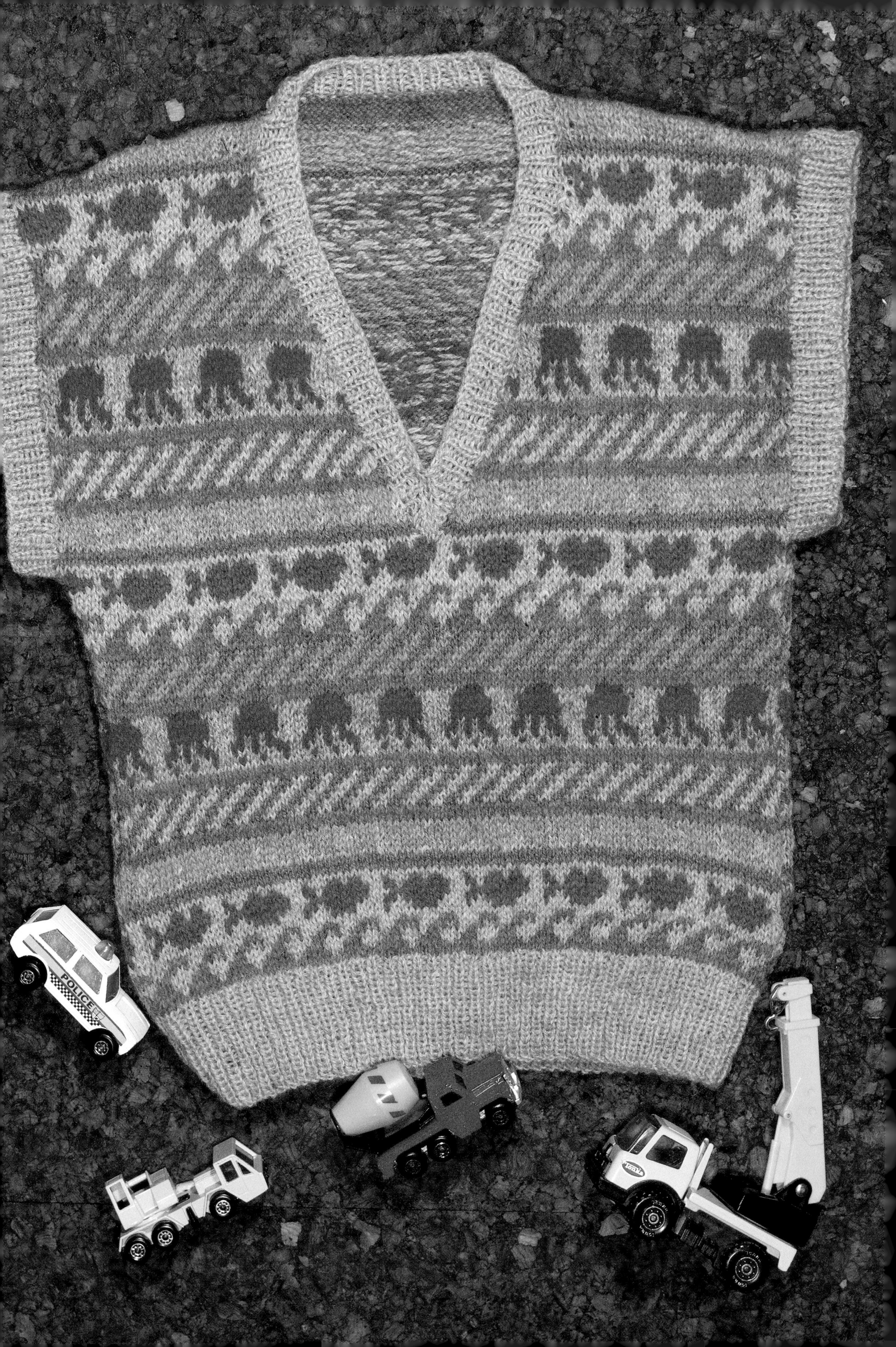
POLICE

Bunny Rabbits jumper

Pattern repeat 8 sts and 16 rows

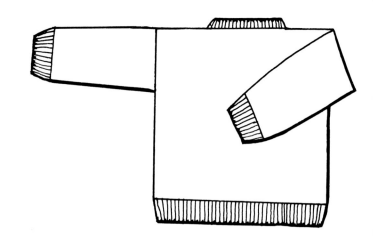

Sizes
To fit 61[71]cm (24[28]in) chest.
Length 37[42]cm (14½[16½]in).
Sleeve length 29[36]cm (11½[14]in).

Materials
6[7] 1oz balls of Mohair (white).
1 skein each of Shetland 2 ply wool in
5 contrast colours (pink, pale green,
bright green, blue, yellow).
Pair 2¾mm (No 12) needles.
Pair 3¾mm (No 9) needles.

Tension
25 sts and 29 rows to 10cm (4in) over
patt worked on 3¾mm needles.

BACK AND FRONT (both alike)
With 2¾mm needles and 1st contrast
(pink) cast on 78[94] sts.
Work for 2 rows in K1, P1 rib.
Change to 2nd contrast (pale green)
and continue in rib for 7 rows, increasing 11 sts evenly in last row
(89(105] sts).
Change to 3¾mm needles.
Work in patt from chart until 6[7] patt
reps have been completed.
Work 2 rows in 3rd contrast (bright
green).

NECK
Cast off 20[20] sts at beginning of
next 2 rows.
Work neck on remaining 49[65]
centre sts.
With 2¾mm needles and 2nd contrast (pale green) work in K1, P1 rib
for 4 rows.
Change to 1st contrast (pink) and
work 2 more rows in rib. Cast off.

SLEEVES
With 2¾mm needles and 1st contrast
(pink) cast on 54[62] sts. Work in K1,
P1 rib for 12[16] rows. Increase 11 sts
evenly along last row (65[73] sts).
Change to 3¾mm needles and work
in patt for 4[5] bunny rabbit repeats,
inc each end of every 17 rows until
there are 73[83] sts.
Work 2 more rows in patt. Cast off.

TO MAKE UP
Do not press because of Mohair
content.
Join shoulder seams.
Sew in sleeves.
Join side and sleeve seams.
Fold side edges of front neck ribbing
diagonally over back neck and slip
stitch along back neck line.
Stitch back neck ribbing in same way
to inside front neck.

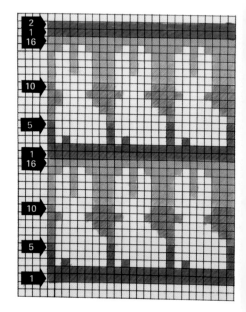

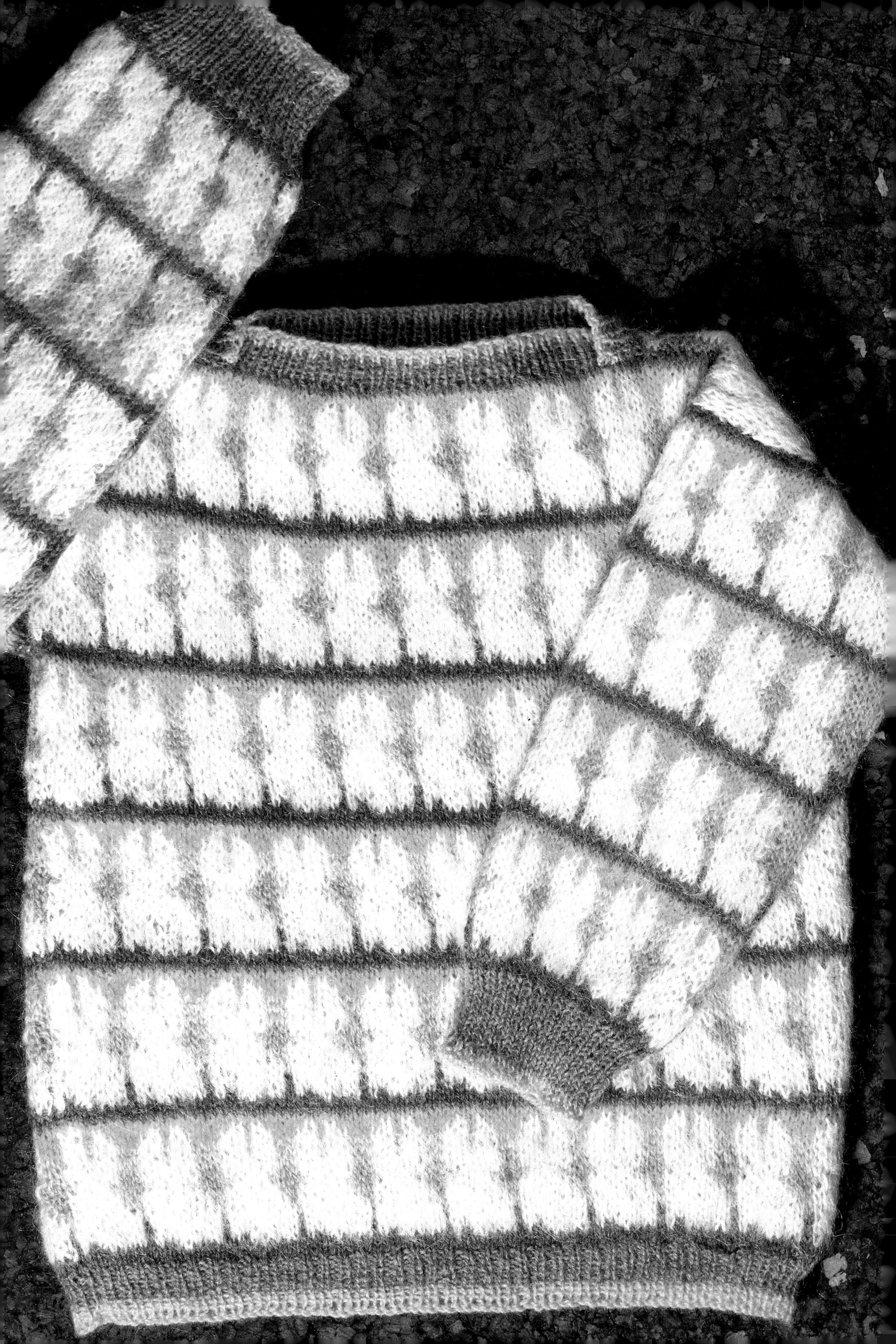

Planes jumper

Pattern repeat 8 sts and 64 rows

Sizes
To fit 61[71]cm (24[28]in) chest.
Length 46[51]cm (18[20]in).
Sleeve length 33[38]cm (13[15]in).

Materials
6 skeins of Shetland 2 ply wool in main colour (beige).
2 skeins each of 2 contrast colours (red, blue).
1 skein each of 3 contrast colours (green, yellow, orange).
Pair 2¾mm (No 12) needles.
Pair 3¼mm (No 10) needles.
Set of 4 2¾mm (No 12) needles.

Tension
30 sts and 34 rows to 10cm (4in) over patt worked on 3¼mm needles.

BACK
With 2¾mm needles and 1st contrast (red) cast on 100[116] sts, work 2 rows in K1, P1 rib.
Change to main colour (beige).
Continue to work in K1, P1 rib, until 6cm (2¼in) have been worked from beg.
Change to 3¼mm needles and st st.
K row. Pick up 9 sts evenly along this row (109[125] sts).
Next row: P to end.*
Work from patt on chart starting at row 1[49].
Put a marker thread between rows 64 & 65.
Finish at row 60 on chart (omitting plane wingtips) 124[140] rows from beg of patt worked.
Cast off 8[10] sts at beg of next 4 rows.
Cast off 10[12] sts at beg of next 2 rows.
Leave rem 57[61] sts on holder.

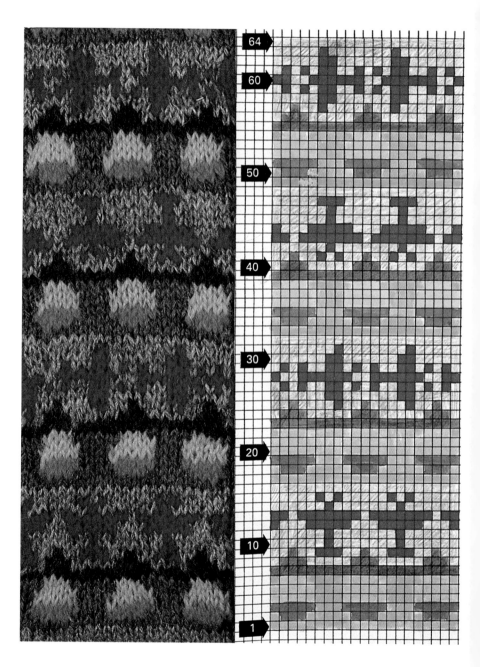

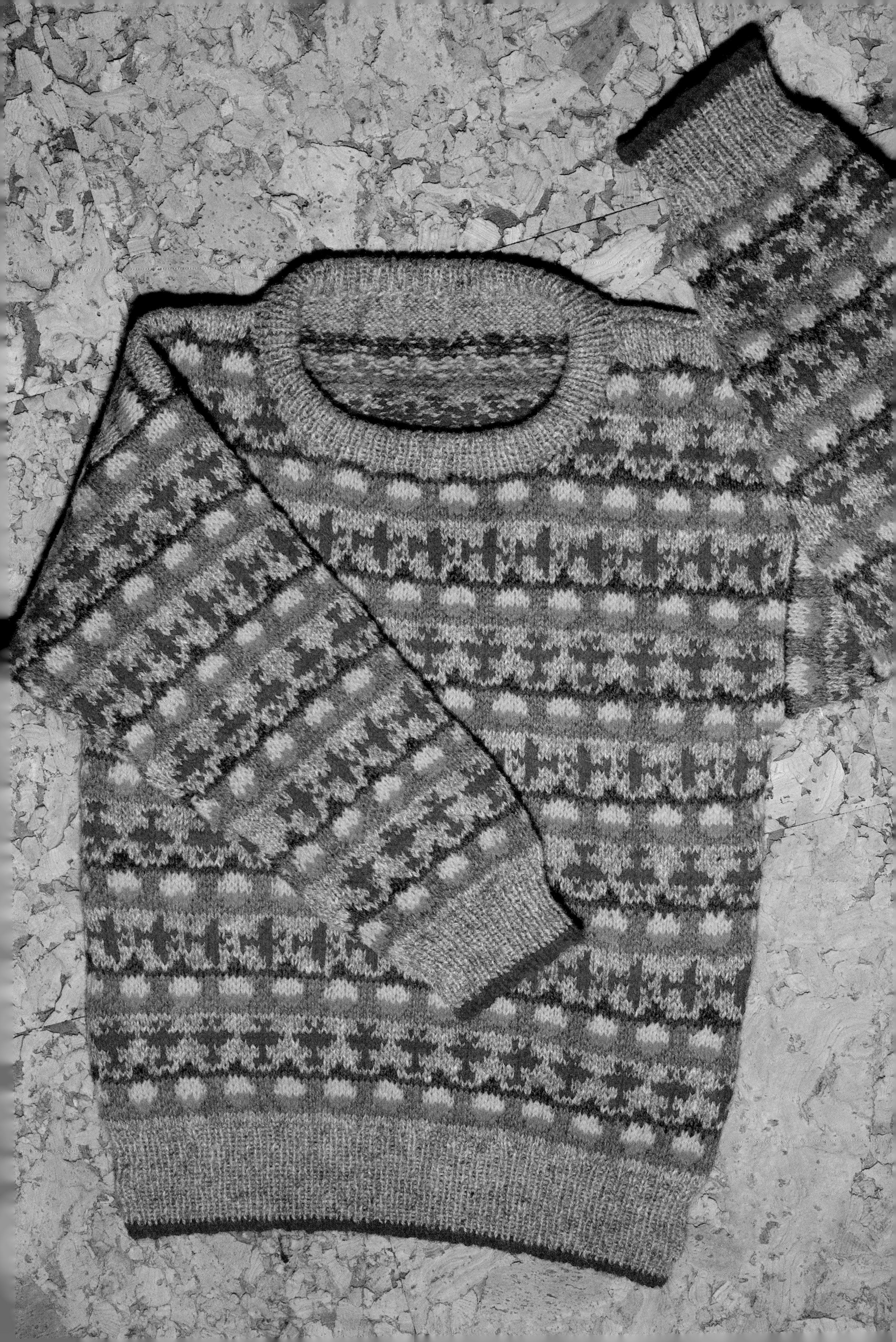

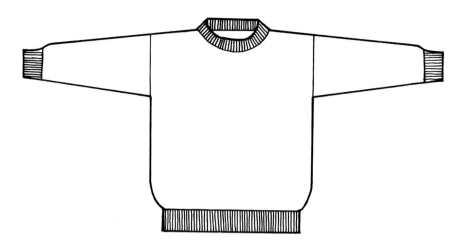

FRONT

Work as for back from beg to *.
Work from patt on chart, putting marker thread between chart rows 64 & 65, finishing with P row, 102 rows from beg of patt worked (row 40 on chart).

Left front

Row 103: K39, turn, leaving rem sts on holder.
Keeping armhole straight, K or P 2 tog on neck edge every row 7 times (32 sts), then K or P 2 tog on every alt row 6 times (26 sts).
Work to row 60 on chart (omitting plane wingtips) 124[140] rows from beg of patt worked.

Cast off 8[10] sts at neck edge. Work to end of row.
Next row: P to end.
Cast off 8[10] sts at neck edge. Work to end of row.
Next row: P to end.
Cast off 10[12] sts. Work to end of row.
Leave centre 31 st on holder.
Complete right side to match left, reversing all shapings.

SLEEVES

Join shoulder seams.
With 3¼mm needles and contrast (green) as used on row 23 of patt on chart, cast on 100 sts.
Work 2 rows st st.

Reverse chart, and work from row 22 of patt down to row 1, then row 64[64] working 5[5] complete planes and balloons.
At the same time decrease 1 st at each end of 12th and every foll 5th row until 68 sts remain (row 1 on chart).

2nd size only
Continue without decreasing in patt from chart row 64 to row 51 (6 complete patts).

Both sizes
Next row: With main colour (beige) P to end.
Next row: K2 tog 9 times evenly along row (60 sts).
Change to size 2¾mm needles, work in K1, P1 rib for 16 rows.
Change to 1st contrast (red), rib 2 more rows.
Cast off.

NECK

With set of 4 2¾mm (No 12) needles and main colour (beige) pick up 25 sts down left front, 31 sts from holder, 25 sts up right front and 56 sts from holder (137 sts). Work 3cm (1¼in) in K1, P1 rib. Cast off.

TO MAKE UP

Press with a damp cloth.
Roll neck inwards and sew to inside. Sew up side seams and sleeve seams starting from rib, taking care to match pattern.

Coco cardigan

Pattern repeat 8 sts and 47 rows

Sizes

To fit 71[76]cm (28[30]in) chest.
Length 43[45.5]cm (17[18]in).
Length of sleeve 34[37]cm
(13½[15]in).

Materials

4 skeins of Shetland 2 ply wool in
main colour (cream).
1 skein each in 6 contrast colours
(white, mustard, blue, green, red,
olive).
2 skeins in 7th contrast colour
(brown).
Pair 2¾mm (No 12) needles.
Pair 3¼mm (No 10) needles.
6 buttons.

Tension

30 sts and 34 rows to 10cm (4in) over
patt worked on 3¼mm needles.

BACK

With 2¾mm needles and main colour
(cream) cast on 101[109] sts.
Work in K1, P1 rib for 10 rows.
Change to 3¼mm needles.
Starting with a K row work from patt
chart for 84 rows.
Place a marker thread at each end of
this row.

1st size only

Work 125 rows (chart row 31). Work
3 more rows in main colour (cream).
Cast off.

2nd size only

Work 129 rows (chart row 35). Cast
off.

Left front

With 2¾mm needles and main colour
(cream) cast on 59[63] sts.
Work in K1, P1 rib for 10 rows.
Leave first 8 sts on holder for button
band.
Change to 3¼mm needles. Starting
with a K row, work from chart for 84

rows (row 37 of chart). Place marker
thread at 84th row.
Work to end of row 115.
Row 116: Cast off 11 sts. P to end.
K2 tog at neck edge on all rows until
33[37] sts rem.
Work straight until front matches
back (125[129] rows). Cast off.

Right front

With 2¾mm needles and main colour
(cream) cast on 59[63] sts.
Work in K1, P1 rib for 5 rows.

Buttonhole

Rib 3, cast off 3, rib 2.

Next row cast on 3 over 3 cast-off sts.
Rib to end.
Work a further 4 rows in rib.
Leave the 8 buttonband sts on holder.
Work in patt from chart as for left
front reversing all shaping.

BUTTONBAND AND BUTTONHOLES

Left front

Pick up 8 sts from holder, increase
1st at inside edge (9 sts). Work in K1,
P1 rib starting with a P st at beginning of right side of work.

47

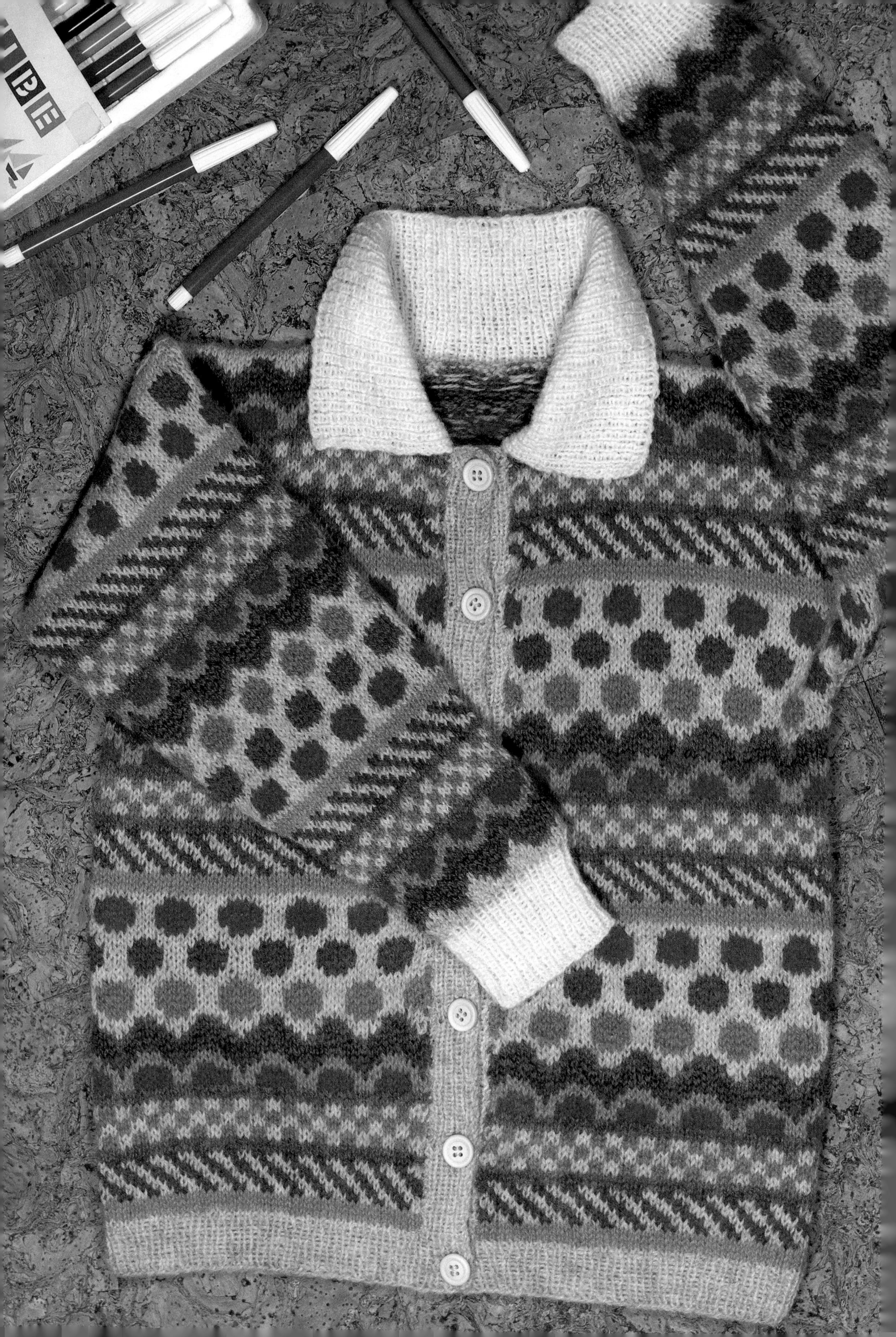

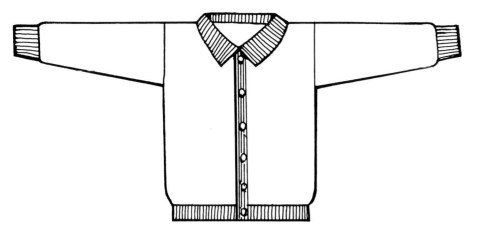

Continue in rib until work is the same length as front, stretching slightly. Do not cast off.

Sew to front and when a few rows from the top, cast off. Finish sewing up.

Right front

Work as for left front making 5 buttonholes evenly spaced, the last starting 1cm from the top. To work buttonholes, rib 3, cast off 3, rib 3. Next row: Rib 3, cast on 3, rib 3 (9 sts).

SLEEVES

Join both fronts to back at shoulders. With 3¼mm needles and main colour (cream) pick up and K93[101] sts between the markers.

Work 3 rows st st.

Reverse chart and work down from row 36[30] to row 1 for 89[95] rows. On 40th[46th] row and every foll 5th row, K2 tog at each end of row until 73[81] sts rem.

Work straight to row 1 on chart.

Work 1 row in main colour (cream).

Decrease 23[23] sts evenly along next row 50[58] sts.

Change to 2¾mm needles and using 1st contrast (white) work in K1, P1 rib for 16 rows.

Cast off in rib.

COLLAR

With 2¾mm needles and 1st contrast (white) cast on 127[139] sts.

Work for 7½cm (3in) in K1, P1 rib.

Cast off loosely in rib.

TO MAKE UP

Sew up sleeve and side seams, using white yarn on cuff ribbing.

Ease collar round neck and sew with a blind st.

Press on inside of work with a damp cloth (excluding rib).

Sew buttons to match buttonholes.

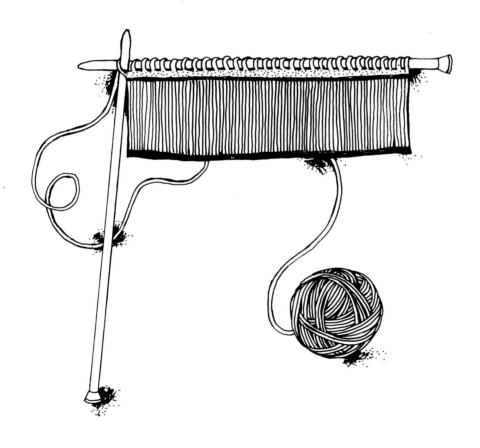

Pansy V neck jumper

Pattern repeat 8 sts and 44 rows

Sizes
To fit 71[76]cm (28[30]in) chest.
Length 50[53]cm (19½[21]in).
Sleeve seam 37[40]cm (14½ [15½]in).

Materials
3 skeins of Shetland 2 ply wool in main colour (navy).
2 skeins each of 6 contrast colours (red, mulberry, blue, beige, green, yellow).
Pair 2¾mm (No 12) needles.
Pair 3¼mm (No 10) needles.

Tension
30 sts and 34 rows to 10cm (4in) over patt worked on 3¼mm needles.

BACK
With 2¾mm needles and 1st contrast (red) cast on 104[120] sts.
Next row: K1, P1 to end.
Next row: Change to main colour (navy). K1, P1, rib.
Continue in K1, P1 rib for 5[7]cm. Inc 1 st in last row (105[121] sts).
Change to 3¼mm needles.
Beg with a K row, work st st in main colour for 2 rows.
Starting at row 1 of chart work in patt for 141[145] rows (row 13[18] of chart).

Shape shoulders
With colour now on needles, cast off 10[12] sts at beg of next 4 rows.
Next row: Cast off 11[13] sts at beg of next 2 rows. Leave rem 43[47] sts on holder for neck back.

LEFT FRONT
Work as given for back until 84 rows have been completed (row 44 on patt chart).
Next row: Patt across 52[60] sts. K2 tog, turn.

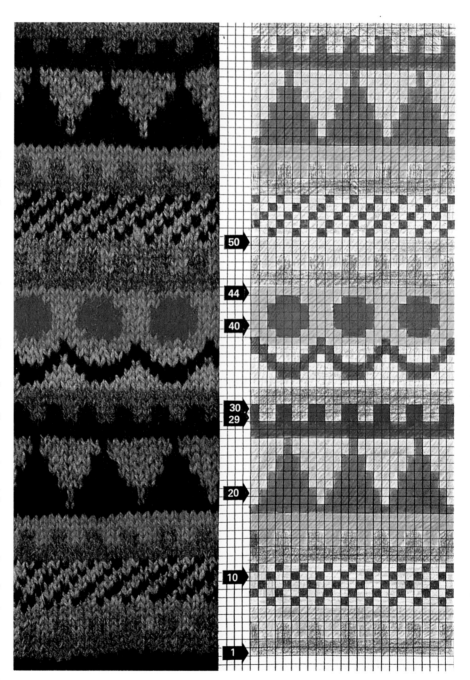

50

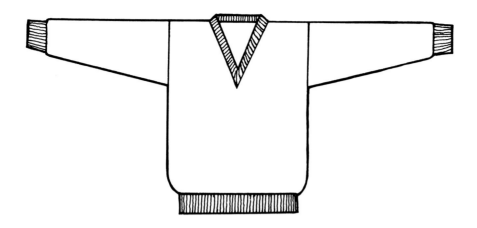

Cont to dec at neck edge every foll alt row until 31[37] sts remain.
Cont in patt without shaping until front measures the same as back (141[145] rows from start).

Shape shoulder

Cast off 10[12] sts at beg of next and foll alt row.
Next row: Cast off rem 11[13] sts.

RIGHT FRONT

Put centre stitch on safety pin.

Complete right side of neck in same way as left, reversing all shapings.

SLEEVES

With 2¾mm needles and 1st contrast (red) cast on 64[68] sts.
Next row: K1, P1 rib.
Next row: Change to main colour (navy). K1, P1 rib for 6[7]cm.
Change to 3¼mm needles and K, inc 10[10] sts in this row (74[78] sts).
Next row: P to end.
Next row: Starting at row 29 of chart,

work in patt, inc 1 st each end of every 6th row until 98[106] sts remain.
Cont in patt until 104[108] rows have been worked ending with row 2[6] of chart.
Cast off.

NECKBAND

Join right shoulder seam.
With right side of work facing, 2¾mm needles and main colour (navy), pick up and K56[58] sts down left side of neck, K centre st from safety pin, pick up and K56[58] sts up right side, K across 43[47] sts from back neck holder (156[164] sts).
Work 2cm in K1, P1 rib, dec 1 st each side of centre front st on every row.
Change to 1st contrast (red).
Work 2 rows in K1, P1 rib, dec as before.
Cast off loosely in rib.

TO MAKE UP

Iron carefully on inside under a damp cloth.
Join left shoulder seam and neckband seam.
Sew in sleeves. Join side and sleeve seams.

Bumble Bees round neck pullover

Pattern repeat 7 sts and 44 rows

Sizes
To fit 71[81:91]cm (28[32:36]in) chest.
Length 51[59:62]cm.

Materials
5 skeins of Shetland 2 ply wool in main colour (mauve).
1 skein each of 7 contrast colours (rust, pale pink, dark green, pale green, dark pink, brown, white).
Pair 2¾mm (No 12) needles.
Pair 3mm (No 11) needles.
Pair 3¼mm (No 10) needles.

Tension
30 sts and 34 rows to 10cm (4in) over st st worked on 3mm needles.

BACK
With 2¾mm needles and 1st contrast (rust) cast on 114[128:144] sts.
Work 2 rows K1, P1 rib.
Change to main colour (mauve) and cont in rib until work measures 8cm, ending with a right side row.
Next row: Rib 8[16:24], (inc in next st, rib 11) 8 times, inc in next st, rib 9[15:23] (123[137:153] sts.).
Change to 3mm needles.
Beg with a K row, cont in st st until back measures 21[27:28]cm from beg, ending with a P row.
Change to 3¼mm needles.
Starting at row 1, work in patt from chart for 46 rows, ending with a P row.
Change back to 3mm needles and main colour (mauve).
Beg with a K row work 2 rows st st.

Shape armholes
Cast off 8 sts at beg of next 2 rows.
Dec 1 st each end of next and every foll alt row until 78[92:108] sts rem.*
Cont without shaping until armholes measure 18[20:22]cm, ending with a P row.

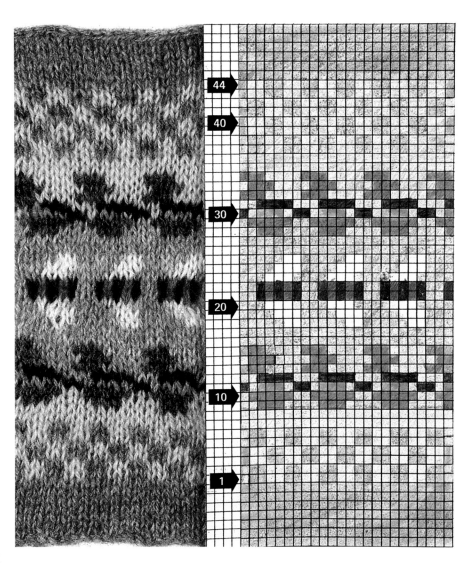

Shape shoulders

Cast off 7[8:9] sts at beg of next 4 rows, then 9[12:14] sts at beg of next 2 rows.
Leave rem 32[36:44] sts for back neck on holder.

FRONT

Work as given for back to start of armhole shaping.
Next row: Cast off 8 sts, at beg of next 2 rows.
Next row: P to end.
Dec 1 st each end of next and every foll alt row until 78[92:108] sts rem.*
Work 2 more rows.

Shape neck

K26[33:41], K2 tog, turn.
Cont to dec at neck edge until 20[27:35] sts rem.
Cont without shaping until front measures same as back to shoulder, ending at armhole edge.

Shape shoulder

Cast off 7[8:9] sts at beg of next and foll alt row.
Cast off rem 9[12:14] sts.
With right side of work facing, slip 24 sts from centre front onto holder.
Rejoin yarn to rem 27[34:42] sts.
K2 tog, K to end.

Complete right side of neck to match left, reversing all shaping.

NECKBAND

Join right shoulder seam.
With right side of work facing, 2¾mm needles and main colour (mauve) pick up 36[44:52] sts down left side of neck, 24 sts from holder, pick up and K36[44:52] sts up right side of neck and 32[36:44] sts from back neck (128[148:172] sts).
Work 6 rows K1, P1 rib, in main colour (mauve).
Change to 1st contrast (rust). Work 2 more rows in rib.
Cast off in rib.

ARMBANDS

Join left shoulder seam and neck-band.
With right side of work facing, 2¾mm needles and main colour (mauve) pick up and K113[121:129] sts.
Work 6 rows in K1, P1 rib.
Change to 1st contrast (rust). Work 2 rows in rib.
Cast off in rib.

TO MAKE UP

Iron on inside under a damp cloth.
Join side seams, taking care to match pattern.

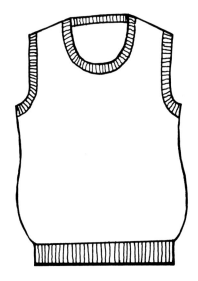

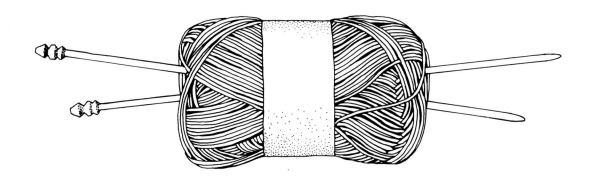

Butterflies V neck pullover

Pattern repeat 8 and 16 sts and 44 rows

Sizes
To fit 71[81:91]cm (28[32:36]in) chest.
Length 51[59:62]cm.

Materials
5 skeins of Shetland 2 ply wool in main colour (light green).
1 skein each of 7 contrast colours (turquoise green, peach, dark green, white, brown, violet, mauve).
Pair 2¾mm (No 12) needles.
Pair 3mm (No 11) needles.
Pair 3¼mm (No 10) needles.

Tension
30 sts and 34 rows to 10cm (4in) over st st worked on 3mm needles.

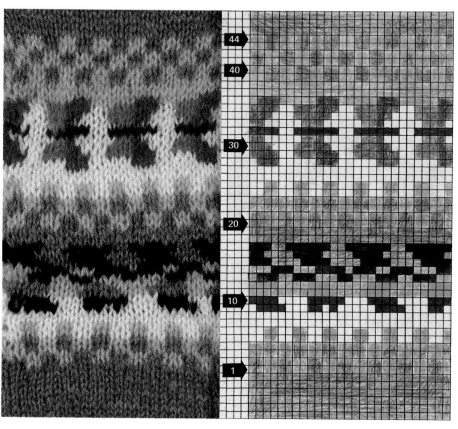

BACK
With 2¾mm needles and 1st contrast (turquoise green) cast on 114[128:144] sts.
Work 2 rows K1, P1 rib.
Change to main colour (light green) and cont in rib until work measures 8cm (3in), ending with a right side row.
Next row: Rib 8[16:24], (inc in next st, rib 11) 8 times, inc in next st, rib 9[15:23] (123[137:153] sts).
Change to 3mm needles.
Beg with a K row, cont in st st until back measures 19[25:26]cm from beg, ending with a P row.
Change to 3¼mm needles.
2nd, 3rd sizes
Increase 1 st each end of next row.
All sizes
Starting at row 1, work in patt from chart for 44 rows.
2nd, 3rd sizes
Decrease 1 st each end of next row.
All sizes
Change back to 3mm needles and main colour.
Beg with a K row work 2 rows st st.

Shape armholes
Cast off 4 sts at beg of next 4 rows.
Dec 1 st each end of next and every foll alt row until 89[101:113] sts rem.
Cont without shaping until armholes measure 18[20:22]cm, ending with a P row.

Shape shoulders
Cast off 7[8:9] sts at beg of next 4 rows, then 9[12:14] sts at beg of next 2 rows.
Cast off rem 43[45:49] sts for back neck.

FRONT
Work as given for back to start of armhole shaping.

Shape neck and armholes
Cast off 4 sts, K57[64:72] (incl st on needle), turn, leaving rem sts on holder.
Complete left side of neck first.
Next row: P to end.
Next row: Cast off 4 sts, K to last 2 sts, K2 tog.
Next row: P to end.
Dec 1 st each end of next and every foll alt row until 34[39:43] sts rem, then every alt row at neck edge only until 23[28:32] sts rem.
Cont without shaping until front measures same as back to shoulder, ending at armhole edge.

Shape shoulder
Cast off 7[8:9] sts at beg of next and foll alt row.
Cast off rem 9[12:14] sts.
With right side of work facing, slip first of rem sts onto a safety pin,

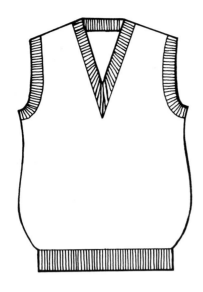

rejoin yarn to rem 61[69:76] sts and K to end.

Complete right side of neck to match left, reversing all shaping.

NECKBAND

Join right shoulder seam.

With right side of work facing, 2¾mm needles and main colour (light green) pick up and K60[64:68] sts down left side of neck, K 1 st from safety pin, pick up and K60[64:68] sts up right side of neck and 42[44:48] sts from back neck (163[173:185] sts).

Work 6 rows K1, P1 rib, working 2 sts tog each side of centre front st on every row.

Change to 1st contrast (turquoise green). Work 2 more rows in rib, dec as before.

Cast off in rib.

ARMBANDS

Join left shoulder seam and neckband.

With right side of work facing, 2¾mm needles and main colour (light green) pick up and K116[124:140] sts.

Work 6 rows in K1, P1 rib.

Change to 1st contrast (turquoise green). Work 2 more rows in rib.

Cast off in rib.

TO MAKE UP

Press carefully on wrong side. Join side seams, taking care to match pattern.

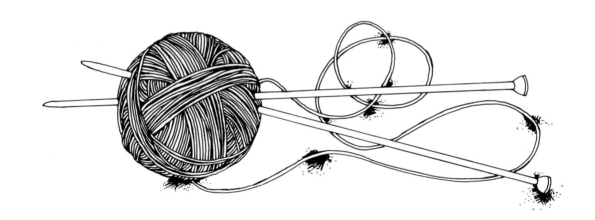

Zigzag pullover

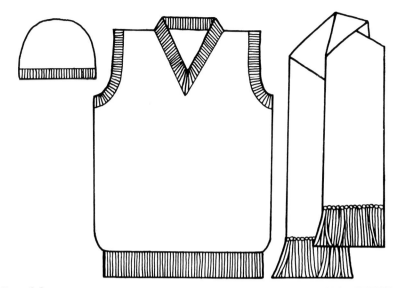

Pattern repeat 10 sts, 6 sts and 37 rows

Sizes
To fit 71[81:91]cm (28[32:36]in) chest.
Length 52[59:62]cm.

Materials
5 skeins of Shetland 2 ply wool in main colour (olive green).
1 skein each of 6 contrast colours (red, dark green, navy blue, green-blue, mulberry, beige).
Pair 2¾mm (No 12) needles.
Pair 3mm (No 11) needles.
Pair 3¼mm (No 10) needles.

Tension
30 sts and 34 rows to 10cm (4in) over st st worked on 3mm needles.

BACK
With 2¾mm needles and 1st contrast (red) cast on 117[131:147] sts.
1st row: K1, *P2, K2, rep from * to last 0[2:2] sts, P0[2:2].
2nd row: K0[2:2], *P2, K2, rep from * to last st, P1.
Change to main colour (olive green).
Rep 1st and 2nd rows 14 times more.
Change to 3mm needles.
Beg with a K row, cont in st st until back measures 21[27:28]cm from beg, ending with a P row.
Change to 3¼mm needles.
Starting with row 1, work in patt from chart for 37 rows.
Change back to 3mm needles and main colour (olive green).
Beg with a P row work 3 rows in st st.

Shape armholes
Cast off 5 sts at beg of next 4 rows.
Dec 1 st each end of next and every foll alt row until 81[89:99] sts rem.
Cont without shaping until armholes measure 19[20:22]cm, ending with a P row.

Shape shoulders
Cast off 7[8:9] sts at beg of next 6 rows.
Cast off rem 39[41:45] sts for back neck.

FRONT
Work as given for back to beg of armhole shaping.

Shape neck and armholes
Cast off 5 sts, K53[60:68] (including st on needle), turn, leaving rem sts on holder.
Complete left side of neck first.
Next row: P to end.
Next row: Cast off 5 sts, K to last 2 sts, K2 tog.
Next row: P to end.
Dec 1 st each end of next and every foll alt row until 31[32:34] sts rem, then every alt row at neck edge only until 21[24:27] sts rem.
Cont without shaping until front measures same as back to shoulder, ending at armhole edge.

Shape shoulder
Cast off 7[8:9] sts at beg of next and foll 2 alt rows.
With right side of work facing, slip first of rem sts onto a safety pin, rejoin yarn to rem 58[65:68] sts and K to end.
Complete right side of neck to match left, reversing all shaping.

NECKBAND
Join right shoulder seam.
With right side of work facing, 2¾mm needles and main colour (olive green) pick up and K60[64:68] sts down left side of neck, K 1 st from safety pin, pick up and K60[64:68] sts up right side of neck and 36[40:44] sts from back neck (157[169:181] sts).
Work 2cm K2, P2 rib, dec 1st each side of centre front st on every row.
Cast off in rib.

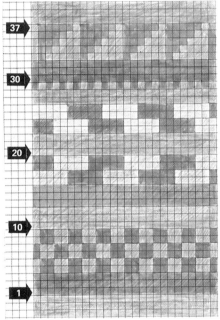

ARMBANDS
Join left shoulder seam and neckband. With right side of work facing, 2¾mm needles and main colour (olive green) pick up and K116[124:140] sts.
Work 2cm K2, P2 rib.
Cast off in rib.

TO MAKE UP
Join side seams, taking care to match pattern.

Zigzag cap & scarf

To match Zigzag pullover, with patt worked in reverse order.

Pattern repeat 10 sts, 6 sts and 63 rows

Sizes
Cap: 46cm (18in) round head, 24cm (9½in) deep.
Scarf: 152cm (60in) long plus 10cm (4in) fringe at each end, 19cm (7½in) wide.

Materials
8 skeins of Shetland 2 ply wool in main colour (olive green).
1 skein each of 6 contrast colours (navy blue, green-blue, dark green, mulberry, red, beige).
Pair 3¼mm (No 10) needles.
Pair 2¾mm (No 12) needles (cap only).

Tension
30 sts and 34 rows to 10cm (4in) over patt worked on 3¼mm needles.

CAP
With 2¾mm needles and main colour (olive green) cast on 143 sts.
1st row: P3, *K2, P2, rep from * to end.
2nd row: *K2, P2, rep from * to last 3 sts, K3.
Work in rib for 20 rows.
Change to 3¼mm needles and work from chart starting at row 1 to row 27.
Work from graph as for scarf but dec each end of row 28 (141 sts).
Cont to work from chart up to row 40.
Row 41: K2 tog, K11, K2 tog, *K12, K2 tog, rep from * to end of row.
Cont to dec for crown keeping chart correct as follows:
Row 42: P to end.
Row 43: *K11, K2 tog, rep from * to end.
Row 44 and every other alt row: P to end.
Row 45: *K10, K2 tog, rep from * to end.

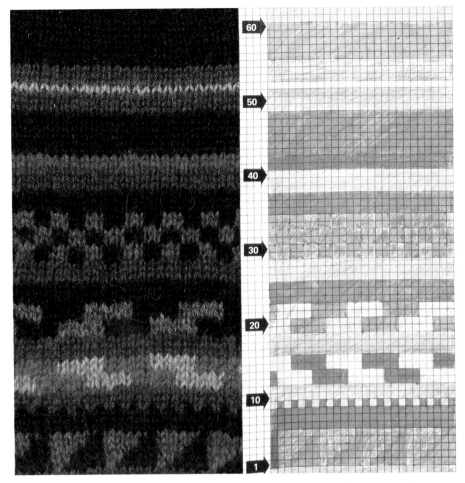

Row 47: *K9, K2 tog, rep from * to end.
Row 49: *K8, K2 tog, rep from * to end.
Row 51: *K7, K2 tog, rep from * to end.
Row 53: *K6, K2 tog, rep from * to end.
Row 55: *K5, K2 tog, rep from * to end.
Row 57: *K4, K2 tog, rep from * to end.
Row 59: *K3, K2 tog, rep from * to end.
Row 61: *K1, K2 tog, rep from * to end.
Row 62: Purl.
Thread yarn from knitting through rem sts and pull through.
Use this yarn to sew up seam.

SCARF
With size 3¼mm needles and main colour (olive green) cast on 143 sts.
Work 14cm in st st.

Begin patt from chart at row 1.
Work to end of chart (row 60).
Change to main colour (olive green).
Cont for 120cm.
Work again from chart, starting with row 60 and wrong side of work facing, working the rows in reverse order.
Comp with 14cm of main colour (olive green).
Cast off.
Press on wrong side of work with damp cloth and fold in half lengthwise.
Sew long edges tog.

TO MAKE TASSELS
Cut lengths of wool 34cm long and use 4 at a time. Using a large crochet hook, thread 4 strands of wool through the end of the scarf and knot, so that 8 strands hang down. Repeat all along both ends of scarf. When all tassels have been knotted, trim to 10cm in length along bottom with a large pair of sharp scissors.

Caterpillars pullover

Pattern repeat 16 sts and 71 rows

Sizes
To fit 71[81:91]cm (28[32:36]in) chest.
Length 45[52:57]cm (17¾[20½:22½] in).

Materials
5[6:6] skeins of 2 ply Shetland wool in main colour (white).
1 skein each of 8 contrast colours (dusty pink, beige, mid green, brown, light green, cinnamon, strawberry, rose pink).
Pair 2¾mm (No 12) needles.
Pair 3¼mm (No 10) needles.

Tension
30 sts and 34 rows to 10cm (4in) over patt worked on 3¼mm needles.

BACK
With 2¾mm needles and main colour (white) cast on 113[129:145] sts.
Work 5cm (2in) in K1, P1 rib.
Change to 3¼mm needles and beg with a K row.
All sizes
K1 row, P1 row with colour now on needles.
1st size only
K1 row, P1 row, K1 row in second contrast (beige).
All sizes
Work in st st in patt from chart starting on 20th[7th:1st] patt row.
Cont in patt until 80[90:96] rows have been worked, ending with a P row.

Shape armholes
Cast off 8 sts at beg of next 2 rows.
Dec 1 st at each end of next and every foll alt row until 85[95:101] sts rem.
Cont in patt without shaping until 135[155:173] rows have been worked in patt.

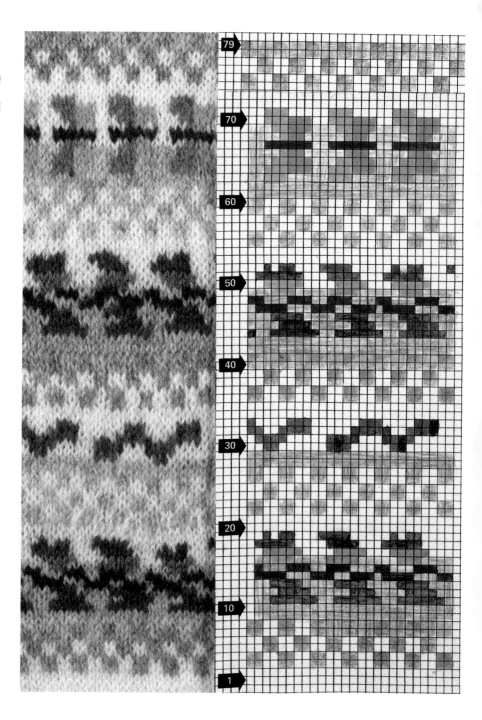

Shape shoulders

Cast off 10[13:14] sts at beg of next 2 rows, then 12[13:14] sts at beg of next 2 rows.

Leave rem 41[43:45] sts on a holder for back neck.

FRONT

Work as for back to beg of armhole shaping.

Shape armholes

Cast off 8 sts at beg of next 2 rows.

Divide for neck

Next row: K2 tog, patt across 46[54: 62] sts, turn and leave rem sts on holder.

Next row: Patt to end.

Dec 1 st each end of next and every foll alt row until 36[40:36] sts rem, ending with a P row.

Cont to dec every alt row at neck edge only until 22[26:28] sts rem.

Cont without shaping until front measures same as back to shoulder, ending at armhole edge.

Shape shoulder

Cast off 10[13:14] sts at beg of next row.

Work 1 row in patt.

Cast off rem 12[13:14] sts.

Leaving centre V st on safety pin, rejoin yarn to rem sts and complete to match 1st side of neck, reversing all shaping.

NECKBAND

Join right shoulder seam.

With right side facing, 2¾mm needles and main colour (white), pick up and K52[56:58] sts down left side of front neck, 1 st from safety pin, 52[56:58] sts up right side of neck, and K across 41[43:45] sts from back neck (146 [156:162] sts).

Work 8 rows K2, P2 rib dec 1 st each side of centre front st on every row.

Cast off loosely in rib.

ARMBANDS

Join left shoulder and neckband seam.

With right side facing, 2¾mm needles and main colour (white), pick up and K120[128:132] sts evenly round armhole edge.

Work 8 rows K2, P2 rib.

Cast off loosely in rib.

TO MAKE UP

Darn in all ends.

Press pieces lightly on wrong side.

Join side seams taking care to match pattern.

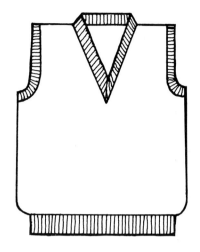

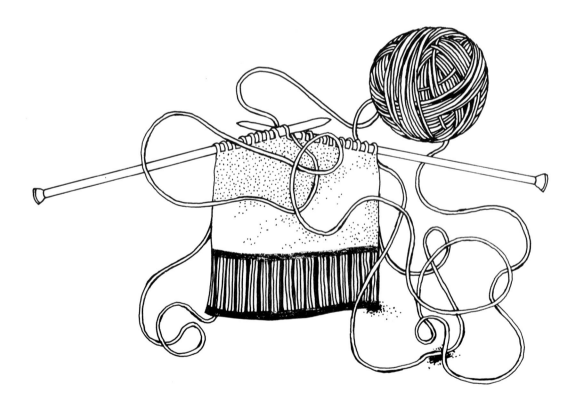

Mushrooms V neck pullover

Pattern repeat 8 sts and 100 rows

Sizes
To fit 71[81:91]cm (28[32:36]in) chest.
Length 56cm (22in).

Materials
4 skeins of Shetland 2 ply wool in main colour (fawn).
1 skein each of 5 contrast colours (orange, red, brown, bright green, dark green).
2 skeins of contrast colour (blue).
Pair 2¾mm (No 12) needles.
Pair 3¼mm (No 10) needles.

Tension
30 sts and 34 rows to 10cm (4in) over patt worked on 3¼mm needles.

BACK
With 2¾mm needles and 1st contrast (orange) cast on 127[137:153] sts.
Work 2 rows in K1, P1 rib.
Change to main colour (fawn) and cont in rib until work measures 6cm, ending with a wrong side row and inc 1 st each end of last row (129 [139:155] sts).
Change to 3¼mm needles. Work 2 rows st st.
Starting at row 1, work in patt from chart for 100 rows.

2nd and 3rd size only
Starting at row 1, begin pattern 3 squares in from edge, so that the mushrooms on row 93 are evenly placed each side of neck shaping.

Shape armholes
Cast off 4 sts at beg of next 4 rows.
Dec 1 st each end of next and every foll alt row until 89[101:113] sts rem.
Cont without shaping until 168 rows from chart have been worked.

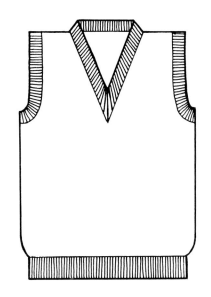

Shape shoulders
Cast off 8[9:11] sts at beg of next 4 rows and 9[11:11] sts at beg of foll 2 rows.
Cast off rem 39[43:47] sts.

FRONT
Work as given for back to beg of armhole shaping.

Shape neck and armholes
Cast off 4 sts, patt across 60[65:73] sts (incl st on needle), turn, leaving rem sts on holder.
Complete left side of neck first.
Next row: Patt to end.
Next row: Cast off 4 sts, patt to last 2 sts, K2 tog.
Next row: Patt to end.
Dec 1 st each end of next and every foll alt row until 33[39:45] sts rem, then every alt row at neck edge only until 25[29:33] sts rem.
Cont without shaping until front measures same as back to shoulder, ending at armhole edge.

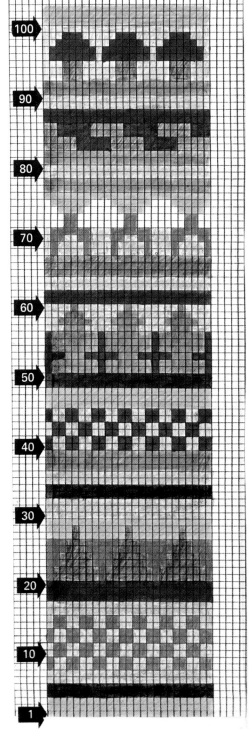

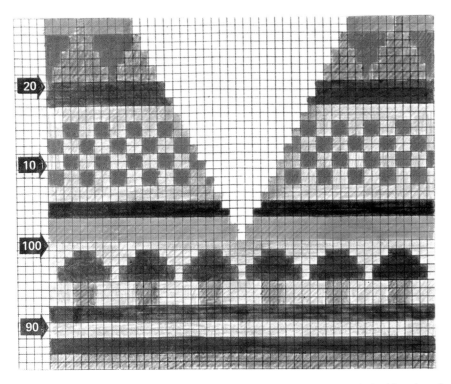

Shape shoulder

Cast off 8[9:11] sts at beg of next and foll alt row.

Cast off rem 9[11:11] sts.

With right side of work facing, slip 1st of rem sts onto a safety pin, rejoin yarn to rem 61[69:76] sts and patt to end.

Complete right side of neck to match left, reversing all shaping.

NECKBAND

Join right shoulder seam.

With right side of work facing, 2¾mm needles and main colour (fawn), pick up and K60 sts down left side of neck, K 1 st from safety pin, pick up and K60 sts up right side of neck and K39[43:47] sts across back neck (160[164:168] sts).

Work 6 rows K1, P1 rib, working 2 sts tog each side of centre front st on every row.

Change to 1st contrast (orange). Work 2 more rows in rib, dec as before.

Cast off in rib.

ARMBANDS

Join left shoulder seam and neckband.

With right side of work facing, 2¾mm needles and main colour (fawn), pick up and K134 sts evenly round armhole edge.

Work 6 rows in K1, P1 rib.

Change to 1st contrast (orange). Work 2 more rows in rib.

Cast off in rib.

TO MAKE UP

Darn in ends.

Press pieces carefully under a damp cloth. Join side seams, taking care to match patterns.

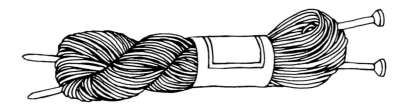

Strawberries waistcoat

*Pattern repeat 8 sts and 16 sts and
85 rows*

Sizes
To fit 76[81:86:91]cm (30[32:34:36]in)
chest.
Length 58cm.

Materials
3[4] skeins of Shetland 2 ply wool in
main colour (light pink).
2 skeins of 1st contrast colour (light
yellow).
1 skein each of 7 contrast colours
(light green, dark green, light brown,
dark brown, blue, rust, rose).
Pair 2¾mm (No 12) needles 35cm
long.
One 2¾mm circular needle 45cm
long (or set of 4).
Pair 3¼mm (No 10) needles 35cm
long.
5 buttons.

Tension
30 sts and 34 rows to 10cm (4in) over
patt worked on 3¼mm needles.

POCKET LININGS
With 3¼mm needles and main colour
cast on 29 sts.
Beg with a K row work 30 rows st st.
Leave sts on spare needle.
Work 2nd lining in same way.

BACK AND FRONTS (worked
in one piece to armholes)
With 2¾mm circular needle and
main colour (pink) cast on 234[250:
266:282] sts.
Work 4cm in K1, P1 rib, ending with a
wrong side row and inc 1 st at end of
last row (235[251:267:283] sts).
Change to 3¼mm circular needle.
Beg with a K row work 2 rows in st st.
Work the first 30 rows of patt as given
in chart.

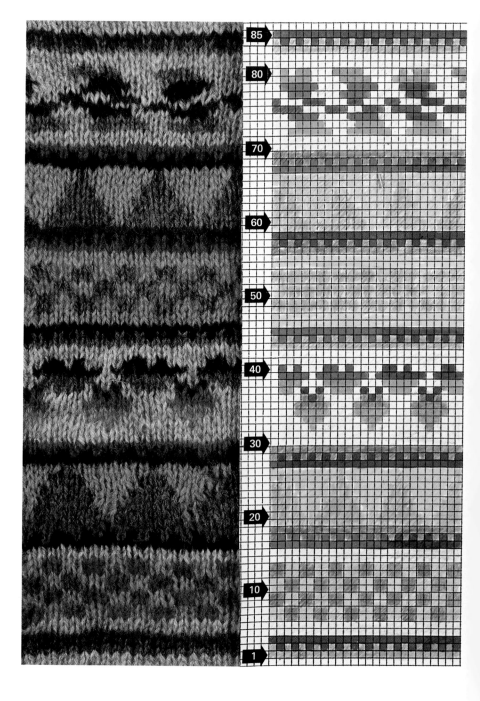

Insert pockets

Patt across 23[27:31:35] sts, slip next 29 sts on to a length of thread, patt across 1st set of pocket lining sts on spare needle, patt to last 52[56:60:64] sts, slip next 29 sts on to a length of thread, patt across 2nd set of pocket lining sts, patt to end.
Cont in patt until 100 rows of patt have been worked from chart.

Shape front neck

Dec 1 st each end of next and every alt row 5 times (225[241:257:273] sts).

Divide for armholes

Next row: Keeping patt correct, K2 tog, patt across 40[44:48:52] sts, turn and leave rem sts on holder.
Next row: Patt to end of row.
Dec 1 st each end of next and every alt row 4 times.
Keeping armhole edge straight cont to dec at neck edge every alt row until 26[30:34:38] sts rem.
Work a further 45 rows in patt from chart, ending at armhole edge.
Cast off 9[10:11:12] sts at beg of next and foll alt row.
Work 1 row in patt.
Cast off rem 8[10:12:14] sts.
Rejoin yarn to rem sts, cast off first 21 sts for armhole, patt across next 99[107:115:123] sts, turn, leaving rem sts on holder.
Dec 1 st each end of next and foll 3

alt rows (91[99:107:115] sts).
Cont in patt without shaping until back measures same as front to shoulder.

Shape shoulders

Cast off 9[10:11:12] sts at beg of next 4 rows, then 8[10:12:14] sts at beg of next 2 rows.
Cast off rem 39 sts.
Rejoin yarn to rem 63[67:71:75] sts, cast off first 21 sts for 2nd armhole, patt to end.
Complete 2nd front to match first, reversing all shaping.

ARMBANDS

Join shoulder seams.
With right side facing, 2¾mm circular needle and main colour, pick up and K 144 sts evenly round armhole.
Work in K1, P1 rib for 8 rows.
Cast off loosely in rib.

NECKBAND

With 2¾mm needles and main colour cast on 12 sts.
Work in K1, P1 rib for 4 rows.
Next row: Rib 5, cast off 3 sts, rib to end.
Next row: Rib to end, cast on 3 sts over those cast off in previous row.
Cont in rib, working 4 more buttonholes 7.5cm apart. Cont in rib until strip is long enough to go right round neck edge.
Cast off.

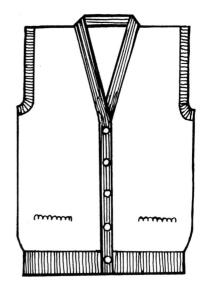

POCKET TOPS

With right side facing, 2¾mm needles and contrast colour yarn to match background colour of strawberries, pick up and K 29 sts from pocket top.
Work 2 rows in st st.
Next row (wrong side): P1, *yrn, P2 tog, rep from * to end.
Beg with a K row, work 3 rows in st st.
Cast off.

TO MAKE UP

Sew on neckband. Sew on buttons. Fold pocket tops to wrong side and slip stitch into place.

Tottie V neck jumper

Pattern repeat 8 sts and 176 rows

Sizes
To fit 81[86]cm (32[34]in) chest.
Length 56[57]cm (22[22½]in).
Sleeve seams 41[41]cm (16in).

Materials
3 skeins of Shetland 2 ply wool in main colour (mauve).
2 skeins each of 3 contrast colours (light green, dark green, dark rust).
1 skein each of 5 contrast colours (yellow, bottle green, blackberry, pale pink, deep pink).
Pair 2¾mm (No 12) needles.
Pair 3¼mm (No 10) needles.

Tension
30 sts and 34 rows to 10cm over patt worked on 3¼mm needles.

BACK
With 2¾mm needles and 1st contrast (yellow) cast on 129[137] sts.
Next row: K1, *P1, K1, rep from * to end.
Change to main colour (mauve).
1st row: P1, *K1, P1, rep from * to end.
2nd row: K1, *P1, K1, rep from * to end.
Rep last 2 rows until work measures 6[7]cm ending with a wrong side row.
Change to 3¼mm needles and main colour (mauve).
Beg with a K row, work 1 row st st in main colour.
Starting at row 16 of chart, work in patt for 97 rows, ending on row 112 of chart.

Shape armholes
Cast off 8 sts at beg of next 2 rows *
Cont in patt without shaping until row 176 of chart has been worked.

Shape shoulder
Working in main colour only

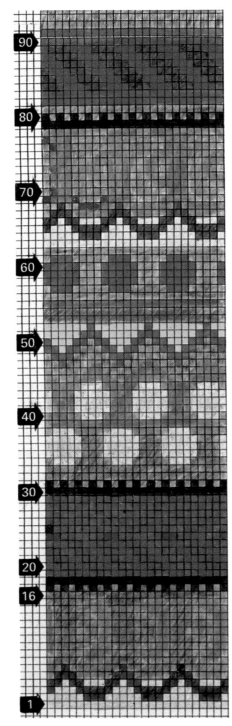

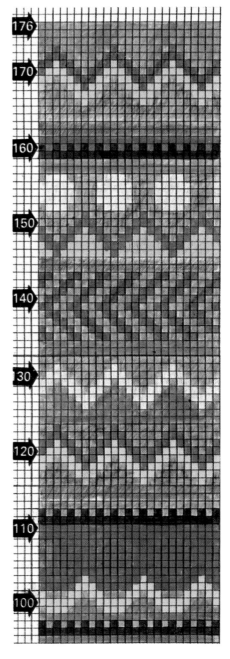

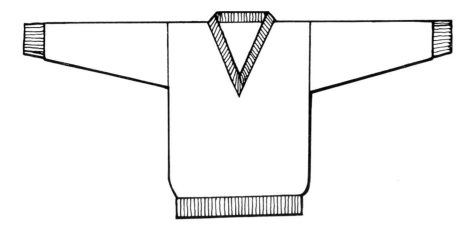

Change to main colour and work in K1, P1 rib until cuff measures 6cm, ending with a right side row.
Next row: Rib 7, (inc in next st, rib 5) 9 times, inc in next st, rib 7 (79 sts).
Change to 3¼mm needles.
Beg with a K row, work 2 rows st st in main colour (mauve).
Starting at row 165 of chart work up to row 176. Starting again at row 1 work in patt inc 1 st each end of every 6th row until there are 109 sts. Cont in patt until 123 rows in patt have been worked, ending with row 111 of chart.
Work one extra row. Cast off.

NECKBAND
Join right shoulder seam.
With right side facing, 2¾mm needles and main colour (mauve) pick up and K54 sts down left side of neck, knit centre front st from safety pin, pick up and K54 sts up right side of neck, K across 47 sts from back neck holder (156 sts).
Work 2cm K1, P1 rib dec 1 st each side of centre front st on every row.
Change to 1st contrast colour (yellow).
Work 1 row in rib, dec as before.
Cast off loosely in rib.

TO MAKE UP
Join left shoulder seam and neckband seam.
Sew in sleeves. Join side and sleeve seams.

(mauve), cast off 11[12] sts at beg of next 4 rows. Cast off 11[13] sts at beg of next 2 rows.
Leave rem 47 sts on holder for back neck.

FRONT
Work as for back to *
Next row: Patt across 56[60] sts, K2 tog, turn and leave rem sts on holder. Cont to dec at neck edge every foll alt row until 33[37] sts rem.
Cont without shaping until front measures the same as back (row 176) ending at armhole edge.

Shape shoulder
Working in main colour (mauve) cast off 11[12] sts at beg of next 2 alt rows.
Cast off 11[13] sts at beg of foll alt row.
Slip 1st st on holder onto safety pin. Rejoin yarn to rem sts, K2 tog, patt to end.
Complete 2nd side of neck to match first, reversing all shaping.

SLEEVES (both sizes alike)
With 2¾mm needles and 1st contrast cast on 69 sts. Work 1 row K1, P1 rib.

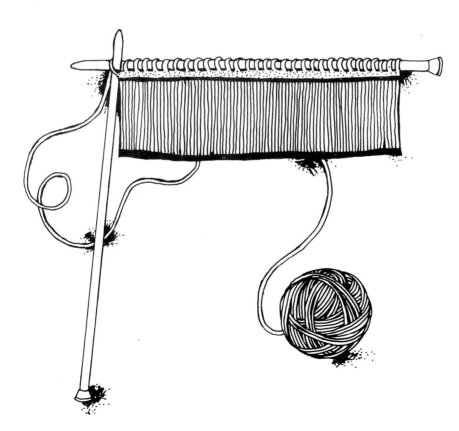

Charity baggy pullover

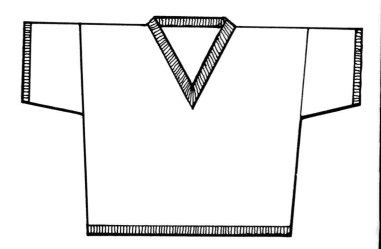

Pattern repeat 8 sts and 30 rows

One size
To fit 86–102cm (34–40in).
Width 54.5cm (21½in).
Length 54.5cm (21½in).
Sleeve seam 14cm (5½in).

Materials
9 skeins of Shetland 2 ply wool in
main colour (purple).
1 skein each of 4 contrast colours
(emerald, ochre, rust, dark green).
Pair 2¾mm (No 12) needles.
Pair 3¼mm (No 10) needles or one
size finer.

Tension
30 sts and 34 rows to 10cm (4in) over
patt worked on 3¼mm needles.

BACK
With 2¾mm needles and main colour
(purple) cast on 161 sts.
Work 4 rows in K1, P1 rib.
Change to 3¼mm needles.
K1 row, P1 row.
Change to 1st contrast colour
(emerald). Beg at row 13 of chart,
patt to end of design. Work in st st in
main colour (purple) until work
measures 54cm.
Cast off.

Left front
Work as for back for 34cm, ending
with P row.
To dec for V, K80, turn.
Dec 1 st at neck edge of each row
until 50 sts remain.
Cont straight for 5cm.
Cast off.

Right front
Leave centre st on safety pin.
Work as for left front, reversing
shaping.

SLEEVES
With 1st contrast (emerald) and
2¾mm needles cast on 125 sts.
K1, P1 rib for 2 rows.
Change to main colour (purple).
K1, P1 rib for 1 row.
Change to 3¼mm needles.
K1 row, P1 row twice (4 rows).
Beg at 1st row of chart, work in patt
to end of design (30 rows), at the
same time inc at beginning of each
row.
Continue in main colour (purple), inc
1 st at beg of each row until 161 sts.
Cast off.

NECKBAND
Join right shoulder seams.

With right side of work facing, 2¾mm
needles and main colour (purple),
pick up and K74 sts down left side of
neck, K st from safety pin, pick up
and K74 sts up right side of neck and
K60 sts from back neck (209 sts).
Work 5 rows K1, P1 rib, working 2 sts
tog each side of centre st on every
row.
Change to 1st contrast (emerald).
Work 2 rows, continuing to dec.
Cast off in rib.

TO MAKE UP
Join left shoulder seam.
Press lightly under damp cloth.
Sew in sleeves.
Join side seams.

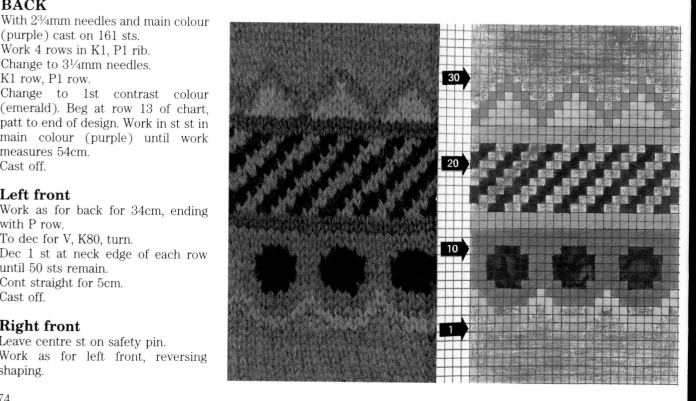

Waves V neck pullover

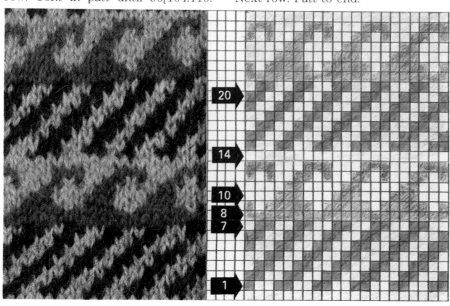

Pattern repeat 6 sts and 14 rows

Sizes
To fit 71[81:91:102]cm (28[32:36: 40]in) chest.
Length 60[62:64:66]cm.

Materials
4[4:5:5] skeins of Shetland 2 ply wool in main colour (beige).
2 skeins each of 3 contrast colours (olive, light green, dark green).
Pair 2¾mm (No 12) needles.
Pair 3¼mm (No 10) needles.

Tension
30 sts and 34 rows to 10cm (4in) over patt worked on 3¼mm needles.

BACK
With 2¾mm needles and 1st contrast (olive) cast on 114[130:146:162] sts.
Work 2 rows in K1, P1 rib.
Change to main colour (beige).
Work 5cm in K1, P1 rib inc 1 st in last row (115[131:147:163] sts).
Change to 3¼mm needles and beg with a K row, work in patt from chart starting on the 1st[8th:1st:8th] patt row. Cont in patt until 96[104:110:

118] rows have been worked, ending with a P row.

Shape armholes
Cast off 8 sts at beg of next 2 rows.
Dec 1 st each end of next and every foll alt row until 85[93:103:111] sts rem.
Cont in patt without shaping until 166[178:188:200] rows have been worked.

Shape shoulders
Cast off 10[12:14:15] sts at beg of next 2 rows, then 12[13:15:16] sts at beg of next 2 rows.
Leave rem 41[43:45:49] sts on a holder for back neck.

FRONT
Work as for back to beg of armhole shaping.

Shape armholes
Cast off 8 sts at beg of next 2 rows.

Divide for neck
Next row: K2 tog, patt across 47[55:63:71] sts, turn and leave rem sts on holder.
Next row: Patt to end.

Dec 1 st each end of next and every foll alt row until 35[35:37:37] sts rem, ending with a P row.
Cont to dec every alt row at neck edge only until 22[25:29:31] sts rem.
Cont without shaping until front measures same as back to shoulder, ending at armhole edge.

Shape shoulder
Cast off 10[12:14:15] sts at beg of next row.
Work 1 row in patt.
Cast off rem sts.
With right side of work facing, slip 1 st of rem sts onto a safety pin, rejoin yarn to rem sts and complete to match 1st side of neck, reversing all shaping.

NECKBAND
Join right shoulder seam.
With right side facing, 2¾mm needles and main colour (beige) pick up and K52[56:58:62] sts down left side of front neck, 1 st from safety pin, 52[56:58:62] sts up right side of neck, and K across 41[43:45:49] sts from back neck (146[156:162:174] sts).
Work 6 rows K1, P1 rib dec 1 st each side of centre front st on every row.
Change to 1st contrast (olive) rib 2 rows.
Cast off loosely.

ARMBANDS
Join left shoulder and neckband seam.
With right side facing, 2¾mm needles and main colour (beige) pick up and K120[128:132:140] sts evenly round armhole edge.
Work 6 rows K1, P1 rib.
Change to 1st contrast (olive) rib 2 rows.
Cast off loosely in rib.

TO MAKE UP
Darn in all ends. Press pieces lightly on wrong side. Join side seams.

Checkers V neck pullover

Pattern repeat 8 sts and 117 rows

Sizes
To fit 71[81:91:102]cm (28[32: 36:40]in) chest.
Length 54[58:62:66]cm (21¼[22¾: 24¼:26]in).

Materials
4[6:6:7] skeins of Shetland 2 ply wool in main colour (white).
1 skein each of 3 contrast colours (beige, rust, dark brown).
Pair 2¾mm (No 12) needles.
Pair 3¼mm (No 10) needles.

Tension
30 sts and 34 rows to 10cm (4in) over patt worked on 3¼mm needles.

BACK
With 2¾mm needles and main colour (white) cast on 104[120:136:152] sts.
Work 5cm (2in) in K2, P2 rib.
Change to 3¼mm needles.
K 1 row inc 11 sts evenly along this row (115[131:147:163] sts).
P 1 row.
Work in patt from chart starting on the 27th[19th:7th:1st] patt row.
Work 1 st before patt for selvedge.
Cont in patt until 98[106:118:124] rows have been worked, ending with row 7 of patt from chart.

Shape armholes
Cast off 8 sts at beg of next 2 rows.
Dec 1 st each end of next and every foll alt row until 85[97:103:111] sts rem.
Cont in patt without shaping until 166[180:196:208] rows have been worked in patt.

Shape shoulders
Cast off 10[13:14:15] sts at beg of next 2 rows, then 12[14:15:16] sts at beg of next 2 rows.
Leave rem 41[43:45:49] sts on a holder for back neck.

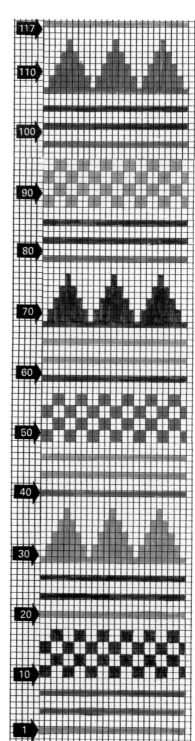

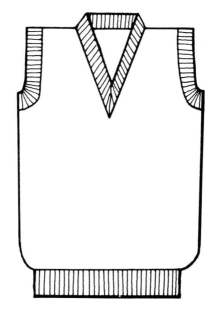

78

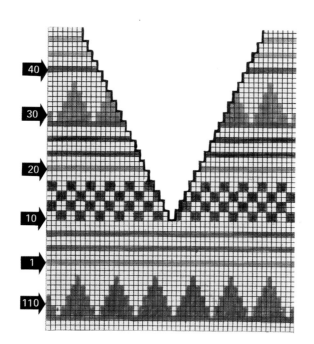

FRONT

Work as for back to beg of armhole shaping.

Shape armholes

Cast off 8 sts at beg of next 2 rows.

Divide for neck

Next row: K2 tog, patt across 47[55:63:71] sts, turn and leave rem sts on holder.

Next row: Patt to end.

Dec 1 st each end of next and every foll alt row until 36[38:38:40] sts rem, ending with a P row.

Cont to dec every alt row at neck edge only until 22[27:29:31] sts rem.

Cont without shaping until front measures same as back to shoulder, ending at armhole edge.

Shape shoulder

Cast off 10[13:14:15] sts at beg of next row.

Work 1 row in patt.

Cast off rem sts.

Leaving centre V st on safety pin, rejoin yarn to rem sts and complete to match first side of neck, reversing all shaping.

NECKBAND

Join right shoulder seam.

With right side facing, 2¾mm needles and main colour (white), pick up and K52[56:58:62] sts down left side of front neck, 1 st from safety pin, 52[56:58:62] sts up right side of neck, and K across 41[43:45:49] sts from back neck (146[156:162:174] sts).

Work 8 rows K2, P2 rib, dec 1 st each side of centre front st on every row.

Cast off loosely in rib.

ARMBANDS

Join left shoulder and neckband seam.

With right side facing, 2¾mm needles and main colour (white), pick up and K120[128:132:140] sts evenly round armhole edge.

Work 8 rows K2, P2 rib.

Cast off loosely in rib.

TO MAKE UP

Darn in all ends. Press pieces lightly on wrong side. Join side seams.

Sissy Pink V neck pullover

Pattern repeat 7 sts and 28 rows; an alternative colour scheme is also shown

Sizes

To fit 81[91:102]cm (32[36:40]in) chest.
Length 54[54:69]cm (23½[23½: 27½]in).

Materials

4[5:6] skeins of Shetland 2 ply wool in main colour (pale pink).
3 skeins in 1st contrast (white).
2 skeins in 2nd and 3rd contrasts (yellow, dark pink).
Pair 2¾mm (No 12) needles.
Pair 3¼mm (No 10) needles.

Tension

30 sts and 34 rows to 10cm (4in) over patt worked on 3¼mm needles.

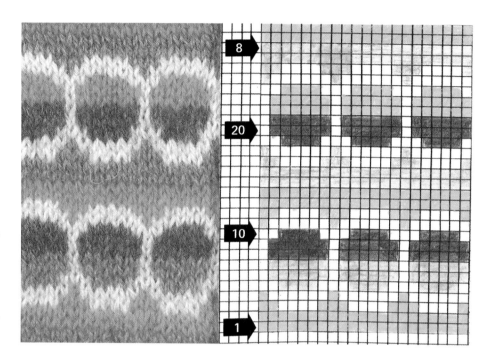

BACK

With 2¾mm needles and main colour (pale pink) cast on 125[139:153] sts.
Work 7cm in K1, P1 rib.
Change to 3¼mm needles.
K1 row, inc 10 sts evenly along this row (135[149:163] sts).
Next row: P.
Work in patt from chart starting at row 15[15:1].
Cont in patt until 110[110:124] rows have been worked.

Shape armholes

Cast off 8 sts at beg of next 2 rows.
Dec 1 st at each end of next and every foll alt row until 97[103:113] sts rem.
Cont in patt without shaping until 71 rows have been worked.

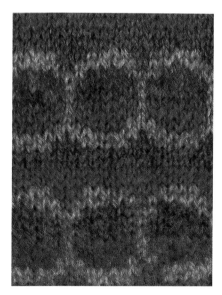

Shape shoulders

Cast off 13[14:16] sts at beg of next 2 rows, then 14[15:16] sts at beg of next 2 rows.
Leave rem 43[45:49] sts on a holder for back neck.

FRONT
Work as for back to beg of armhole shaping.

Shape armholes
Cast off 8 sts at beg of next 2 rows.

Divide for neck
Next row: K2 tog, patt across 57[64:71] sts, leave rem sts on holder.
Next row: Patt to end.
Dec 1 st each end of next and every foll alt row until 37[39:40] sts rem.
Cont to dec until 27[28:32] sts rem.
Work in patt from chart without shaping until front measures the same as back to shoulder, ending at armhole edge.

Shape shoulder
Cast off 13[14:15] sts at beg of next row.
Work one row in patt.
Cast off rem sts.
With right side of work facing, slip 1 st of rem sts onto a safety pin, rejoin yarn to rem sts and complete to match 1st side of neck, reversing all shaping.

NECKBAND
Join right shoulder.
With right side of work facing, 2¾mm needles and main colour (pale pink), pick up and K56 sts down left side of front neck, 1 st from safety pin, 56 sts up right side of neck and K across 43[45:49] sts from back neck (156[158:162] sts).
Work 8 rows in K1, P1 rib, dec 1 st each side of centre front st on every row. Change to 1st contrast (white), rib 2 more rows with decreasing. Cast off loosely in rib.

ARMBANDS
Join left shoulder seam and neckband seam.
With right side of work facing, 2¾mm needles and main colour (pale pink) pick up and K128 sts.
Work 8 rows in K1, P1 rib. Change to 1st contrast (white). K1, P1 for 2 rows. Cast off loosely in rib.

TO MAKE UP
Darn in all ends.
Press pieces lightly on wrong side.
Join side seams.

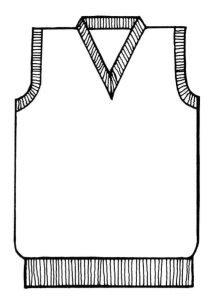

Darts waistcoat

Pattern repeat 7 and 9 sts and 32 rows

Sizes
To fit 81[91:102]cm (32[36:40]in) chest.
Length 63[65:70]cm (25[26½: 27½]in).

Materials
5 skeins of Shetland 2 ply wool in main colour (beige).
2 skeins of 3 contrast colours (blue, yellow, rust).
Pair 2¾mm needles (No 12).
Pair 3¼mm needles (No 10).
6 buttons

Tension
30 sts and 34 rows to 10cm (4in) over patt worked on 3¼mm needles.

BACK
With 2¾mm needles and main colour (beige) cast on 132[146:160] sts.
Work 5cm in K1, P1 rib.
Change to 3¼mm needles.
Beg with a K row, work in patt from chart starting at row 17[17:1] ending with a P row (106[106:122] rows). Row 26 of chart.

Shape armholes
Cast off 10 sts at beg of next 2 rows, then dec 1 st at each end of work until 96[102:110] sts rem.
Cont in patt until 74[77:82] rows from beg of armhole shaping.

Shape shoulder
At beg of next 4 rows cast off 8[9:11] sts, then 9[10:11] sts at beg of next 2 rows. Cast off rem sts.

FRONT

Pocket inset
With 3¼mm needles and main colour (beige), cast on 30[30:35] sts.

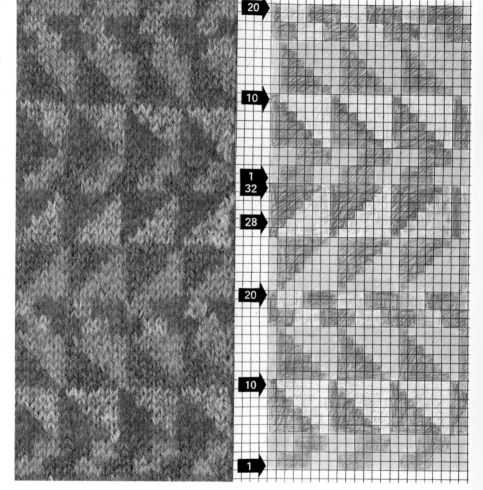

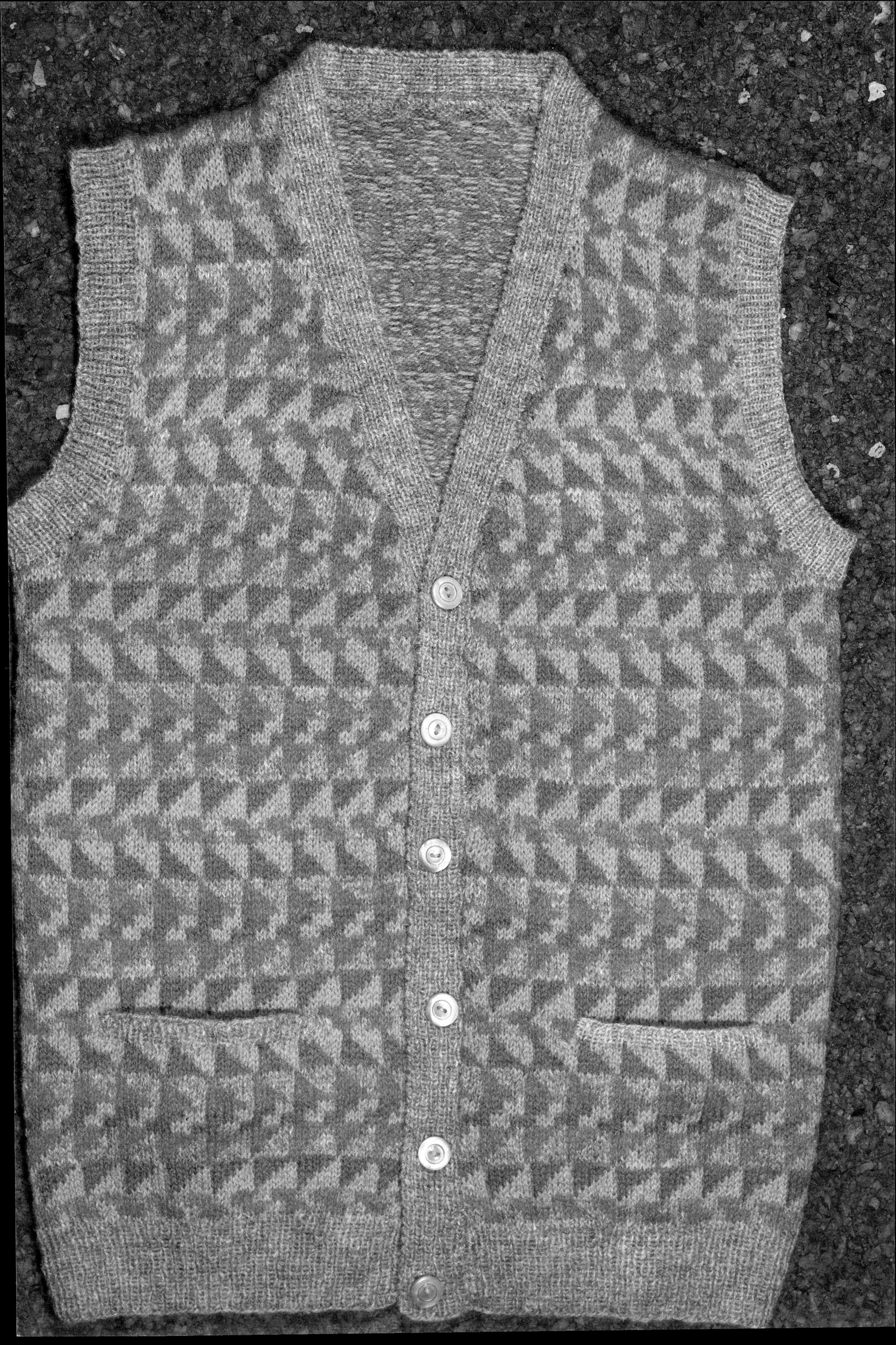

Starting with a K row, work 26[32:31] rows. Leave on holder.
Work 2nd pocket in same way.

Left front
With 2¾mm needles and main colour (beige), cast on 78[86:93] sts.
K1, P1 rib for 4 rows.

Buttonhole
Rib to last 8 sts, cast off next 3 sts, rib 5 sts.
Next row: Rib, casting on 3 sts over cast-off sts.
Rib for next 12 rows (5cm).
With right side facing, rib 13 sts (leave on holder to be knitted up later).
Change to 3¼mm needles.
Beg with a K row, work in patt on chart starting at row 17[17:1] to row 48[48:32].

Pocket
K22[24:27] sts. Slip next 30[30:35] sts onto thread.
Patt across 1st set of pocket lining sts from holder.
Patt to end of row.
Work straight in patt from chart until front measures same as back (row 26 of chart).

Armhole and neck shaping
Cast off 10 sts. K1 row, then dec both ends of next alt rows until 38[38:43] sts rem.

Cont dec at front edge only until 25[29:33] sts rem.
Work in patt until armhole measures same as back (74[77:80] rows from beg of armhole shaping).

Shape shoulder
Armhole edge: Cast off 8[9:11] sts at beg of next and foll alt row.
Cast off rem sts.

Right front
Work in same way as left front, reversing all shapings.

Pocket edges
With 2¼mm needles and main colour (beige), slip pocket sts from thread.
Work 3 rows K1, P1 rib. Cast off in rib.
Sew pocket lining to fronts with invisible sts.
Sew pocket rib in place.
Sew shoulder seams.

RIGHT FRONT BAND
With right side facing, slip 13 sts from holder onto 2¾mm needles. Rejoin main colour (beige).
Rib until band fits up front edge and across back to left shoulder. Cast off, stretching band slightly.

LEFT FRONT BAND
Work left front in the same way making 5 more buttonholes placed evenly up to 1st neck dec.
Work up to left shoulder seam. Cast

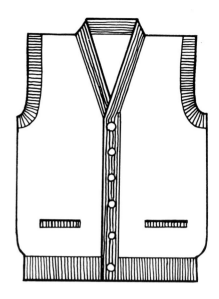

off left front band when edge of right front band is reached.
Join tog.

ARMBANDS
With right side facing, 2¾mm needles and main colour (beige), rejoin yarn. Pick up 128[132:140] sts.
Rib 10 rows.
Cast off in rib.

TO MAKE UP
Press carefully under damp cloth on wrong side of work.
Sew up side seams.
Sew on buttons to correspond with buttonholes.

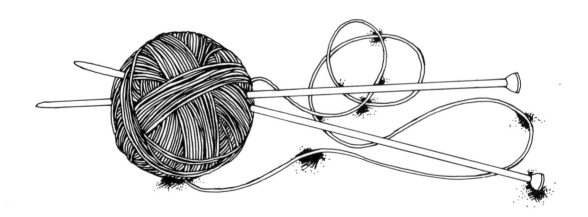

Fall waistcoat

Pattern repeat 8 sts and 57 rows

Sizes
To fit 81[91:102]cm (32[36:40]in) chest.
Length 63[65:70]cm (25[26½: 27½]in).

Materials
4 skeins of Shetland 2 ply wool in main colour (mulberry).
2 skeins each of 2 contrast colours (rust, green).
1 skein each of 3 contrast colours (cinnamon, very dark green, grey-blue).
Pair 2¾mm (No 12) needles.
Pair 3¼mm (No 10) needles.
6 buttons

Tension
30 sts and 34 rows to 10cm (4in) over patt worked on 3¼mm needles.

BACK
With 2¾mm needles and main colour (mulberry), cast on 131[145:161] sts.
Work in K1, P1 rib for 5cm.
Change to 3¼mm needles.
With colour on needle K1 row, P1 row.
Starting with a K row work from patt on chart, beg at row 20[16:1].
Cont in patt until 111[126:130] rows have been completed (row 14 on chart) ending with a P row.

Shape armholes
Cast off 10 sts twice, dec at each end of work until 97[105:113] sts rem.
Cont in patt until 74[77:80] rows from beg of armhole shaping.

Shape shoulder
At beg of next 4 rows, cast off 8[9:11] sts then 9[10:11] at beg of next 2 rows.
Cast off rem sts.

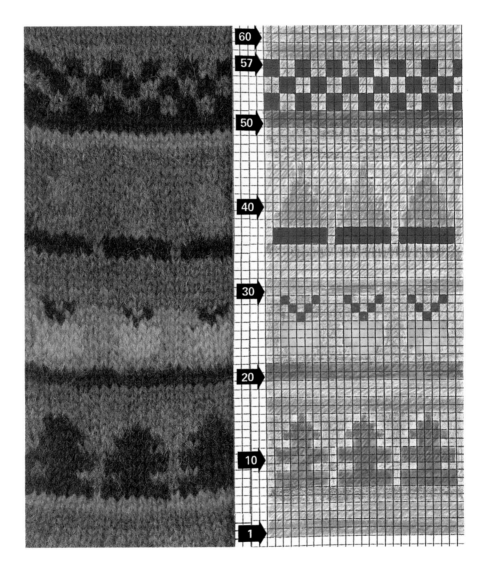

FRONT

Pocket inset

With 3¼mm needles and main colour (mulberry), cast on 30[30:35] sts.
Starting with a K row, work for 26[32:31] rows.
Leave on holder.
Work 2nd pocket in the same way.

Left front

With 2¾mm needles and main colour (mulberry), cast on 78[86:94] sts.
K1, P1 rib for 4 rows.

Buttonhole

Rib to last 8 sts, cast off next 3 sts, rib 5 sts.
Next row: Rib, casting on 3 sts over cast-off sts.
Rib for 12 rows (5cm).
Right side of work. Rib 13 sts (leave on holder to be knitted up later).
With colour on needle, K1 row, P1 row.
Change to 3¼mm needles.
Work from chart, starting at row 20[16:1].

Pocket

Centre edge (chart row 47[47:31]. K 24[24:27] sts. Slip next 30[30:35] sts onto a thread. Patt across 1st set of pocket lining sts on holder, patt to end of row.
Work straight in patt from chart until front measures same as back (row 14 on chart).

Armhole and neck shaping

Cast off 10 sts.
K1 row, then dec both ends of next alt rows until 38[38:43] sts rem.
Cont to dec at front edge only until 25[28:33] sts rem.
Work in patt until armhole measures same as back (74[77:80] rows).

Shape shoulder

Armhole edge: Cast off 8[9:11] sts. K to end.
Next row: P.
Next row: Cast off 8[9:11] sts. K to end.
Next row: P.
Next row: Cast off 9[10:11] sts.

Right front

Work in same way as left front, reversing all shapings.

Pocket edges

With 2¼mm needles and main colour (mulberry), slip pocket sts from thread.
Work 3 rows K1, P1 rib.
Cast off in rib.
Sew pocket linings inside fronts with invisible sts.
Sew pocket rib in place.
Sew shoulder seams.

RIGHT FRONT BAND

With right side of work facing, slip 13 sts from holder onto 2¾mm needles.
Rejoin main colour (mulberry).
Rib until band fits up front edge and across back to left shoulder.
Cast off (stretch slightly for a firm edge).
Work left front in the same way making 5 more buttonholes placed evenly up to first neck dec.
Work up to left shoulder seam. Do not

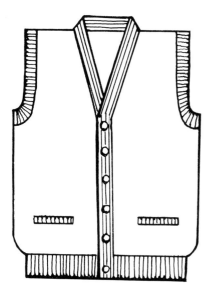

cast off.
Sew bands to waistcoat, cast off left front band when you have reached the edge of right front. Join tog.

ARMBANDS

With right side of work facing, 2¾mm needles and main colour (mulberry), rejoin yarn. Pick up 128[132:140] sts.
Rib 10 rows.
Cast off in rib.

TO MAKE UP

Sew up side seams.
Press carefully on wrong side of work.
Sew on buttons to correspond with buttonholes.

Flower Pots V neck pullover

Pattern repeat 9 and 10 sts and 99 rows

Size
To fit 96cm (36in) chest.
Length from shoulder to waist 69cm (27in).

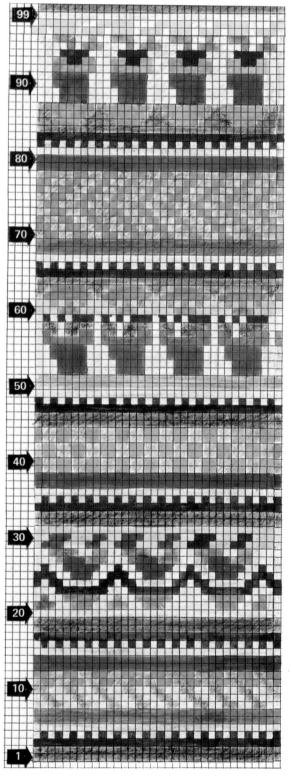

Materials
4 50g balls of double knitting wool in main colour (beige).
2 50g balls of 1st contrast (cinnamon).
1 50g ball of 7 contrast colours (navy, dark green, airforce blue, mustard, rust, bright green, yellow).
Pair 3¾mm (No 9) needles.
Pair 3mm (No 11) needles.

Tension
25sts and 27 rows to 10cm (4in) over patt worked on 3¾mm needles.

BACK
With 3mm needles and 1st contrast (cinnamon) cast on 125 sts and work in double rib.
Row 1: *K2, P2, rep from * to last 3 sts, K3.
Row 2: P3, *K2, P2, rep * to end.
Change to main colour (beige) after 2 rows.
Cont in double rib for 8cm ending with row 2.
Change to 3¾mm needles.
K row. Inc 6 sts evenly along this row (131 sts).
Next row: P.
Cont in st st working from patt on chart until end of row 99.*
Next row: Keeping pattern correct, P to end.
Next row: Cast off 7 sts at beg of next 2 rows.
Cont to K2 tog at beg of each row until 105 sts rem.
Work straight until 156 rows have been completed.
Starting on row 57, cast off 10 sts at beg of next 6 rows.
Leave rem 45 sts on holder.

FRONT
Work as for back to * (beg of armholes).

Shape armholes and neck
Next row: P to end.
Cast off 7 sts at beg of row 101, patt across 58 sts, turn.
Leave rem sts on holder.
Cont to K or P 2 tog at beg of each row until 44 sts rem.
Keeping armhole straight, dec on neck edge only until 30 sts rem.
Cont straight until 156 rows have been completed.
On 157th row cast off 10 sts, work to

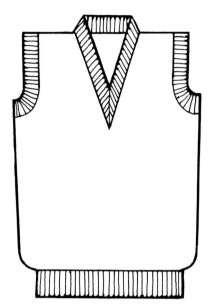

end.
Work 1 row.
Next row: Cast off 10 sts at beg of row, work to end.
Work 1 row.
Cast off.
Rejoin yarn to rem sts. Cast off 7 sts at armhole edge, work to 58 sts in patt, leave rem centre st on safety pin. Complete to match first side of work reversing all shapings.

NECKBAND
Join right shoulder seams.
With 3mm needles and main colour (beige) pick up 60 sts down left front, 1 st from safety pin, 60 sts up right front, 45 sts from back of neck (166 sts).
Mark centre V st with safety pin or thread.
Work in K2, P2 rib as for back.
With right side of work facing, dec each side of centre st.
Work to 2 sts before centre st, sl 1 K or P, psso, K centre st, K or P 2 tog, work to end.
Work for 3cm. Cast off.

ARMBANDS (both alike)
Join left shoulder seam.
With 3mm needles and main colour (beige) pick up 121 sts round armhole.
With right side of work facing, work in K2, P2 rib as for back for 3cm.

TO MAKE UP
Darn in all ends.
Press pieces lightly on wrong side.
Join side seams.

Inca V neck sweater

Pattern repeat 8 and 10 sts and 166 rows

Note
The colour photograph opposite shows Inca worked in double knitting wool. The colour photograph of a swatch of knitting shows the pattern worked in 3 ply Shetland wool in different colours. Choose your own shades or follow either example shown here.

Sizes
To fit 96[102]cm (38[40]in).
Length 64cm (25¼in).
Underarm seam 54cm (21¼in).

Materials
Either:
6[7] 50gm balls of double knitting wool in main colour (maroon).
6[7] 50gm balls in 1st contrast (navy).
3 50gm balls in 2nd contrast (brown).
2 50gm balls in 3rd contrast (black).
2 50gm balls in 4th contrast (grey).
1 50gm ball in 5th contrast (ochre).
Or:
3[4] 2oz skeins of Shetland 3 ply wool in main colour (chestnut).
4 2oz skeins in 1st contrast (navy).
2 2oz skeins in 2nd contrast (cinnamon).
2 2oz skeins in 3rd contrast (black).
1 2oz skein in 4th contrast (blue).
1 2oz skein in 5th contrast (mustard).
Pair 3mm (No 11) needles.
Pair 3¾mm (No 9) needles.

Tension
24 sts and 27 rows to 10cm (4in) over pattern worked on 3¾mm needles.

BACK
With 3mm needles and 1st contrast (navy) cast on 123[139] sts.
Work 8cm (3¼in) in double rib as follows.

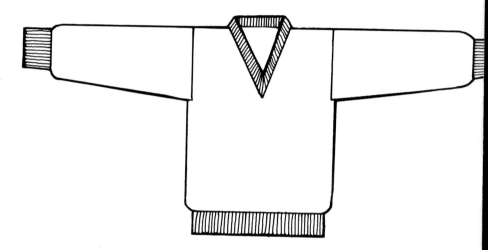

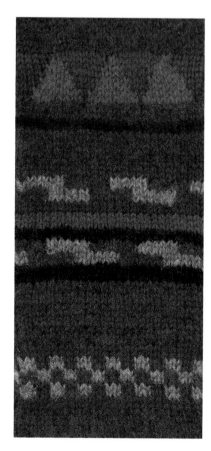

Row 1: P3, *K2, P2, rep from * to end.
Row 2: *K2, P2, rep from * to last 3sts, K3.
End with row 2.
Change to 3¾mm needles and main colour (maroon or chestnut).
Beg with a K row, work in patt from chart starting at row 15.
Cont in patt to row 100.*
Row 101: Cast off 5 sts, K to end.
Row 102: Cast off 5 sts, P to end.
With main colour (maroon or chestnut), cont to work straight until row 167.
Row 167: Cast off 12 sts, K to end.
Row 168: Cast off 12 sts purlwise, P to end.
Cast off 12 sts at beg of next 2 rows.
Cast off rem sts.

FRONT
Work as for back to *.

Left front
Row 101: Cast off 5 sts, K56[64] sts, turn, P to end.
Keep armhole edge straight.
At neck edge of every alt row, K2 tog 18 times until 39[47] sts rem.

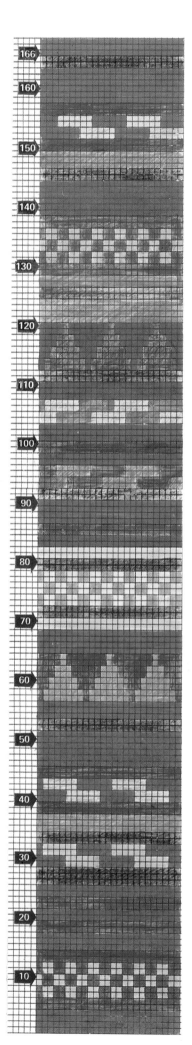

Cont straight until row 167.
Row 167: Cast off 12 sts, K to end.
Row 168: P.
Row 169: Cast off 12 sts, K to end.
Row 170: P.
Cast off rem sts.

Right front
Leaving centre V st on safety pin, rejoin yarn at centre.
Work right front to match left front, reversing all shaping.

SLEEVES (both alike)
With 3mm needles and 1st contrast (navy) cast on 65 sts.
Work 8cm (3¼in) in double rib as follows.
Row 1: P3, *K2, P2, rep from * to last 2 sts, K2.
Row 2: *P2, K2, rep from * to last st, K1.
End with row 2.
Change to 3¾mm needles and main colour (maroon or chestnut).
Inc 10 sts evenly along 1st row (75 sts).

Work from patt to row 54.
Inc at each end of every 5th row until 105 sts on needle.
Cont straight from chart to row 131.
Cast off.

NECKBAND
Join left shoulder seam with main colour (maroon or chestnut).
Pick up 54 sts down left side of neck, pick up 1 st from safety pin, pick up 54 sts up right side of neck, pick up 35 sts from back neck (144 sts).
With 3mm needles and 1st contrast (navy) work in double rib, dec 1 st before centre st and 1 st after centre st on every row.
Work for 3cm (1¼in).
Cast off.

TO MAKE UP
Press with damp cloth on wrong side.
Join right shoulder seam with main colour (maroon or chestnut).
Sew up side seams and underarm seams, starting at rib, using 1st contrast (navy).

Fir Trees waistcoat

Pattern repeat 8 sts and 55 rows

Sizes
To fit 91–97[102–107]cm (36–38 [40–42]in) chest.
Length to armhole 48cm (19in).
Length to shoulder 74cm (29in).

Materials
6oz of Shetland 3 ply wool in main colour (olive).
2oz each of 5 contrast colours (dark brown, dark olive, beetroot red, air-force blue).
5 buttons in main colour.
Pair 4mm (No 8) needles.
Pair 3¼mm (No 10) needles.

Tension
24 sts and 27 rows to 10cm (4in) across patt worked on 3¼mm needles.

POCKET LININGS
With 4mm needles and 1st contrast (dark brown) cast on 27 sts.
Beg with a K row work from patt on chart for 30 rows.
Leave sts on st holder.
Work 2nd lining in same way.

BACK AND FRONTS (worked in one piece to armholes)
With 3¼mm needles and main colour (olive) cast on 232[255] sts.
Work 3cm in P1, K1 rib, ending each row with P1.

Buttonhole
With wrong side of work facing, rib 3 sts, cast off 3 sts, rib to end of row.
Next row: Rib to last 6 sts, cast on 3 sts over cast-off sts, rib 3.
Cont in rib until work measures 7cm. On last row (wrong side of work) rib 7 sts and leave on safety pin, rib to end.
Change to 4mm needles.
Beg with a K row work 25 rows of patt as given in chart.

Insert pockets
Patt across 23 sts, rib 27 sts, work in st st and patt to last 50 sts, rib 27 sts, work in st st and patt to end of row.
Work 3 more rows in this way.
Next row: Patt across 23 sts, cast off 27 sts, work in st st and patt to last 50 sts, cast off 27 sts, work in st st and patt to end of row.
Next row: Patt across 23 sts, patt across 1st set of pocket lining sts, patt to last 50 sts, patt across 2nd set of pocket lining sts, patt to end of row.
Cont to work from graph for 87 rows.
Shape front and armholes.
K2 tog or P2 tog at each end of 88th, 91st and 94th rows. Work 2 more rows.
Row 97: K2 tog, work 48 sts, cast off 9[17] sts, work 103 sts, cast off 9[17] sts, work to last 2 sts, K2 tog.
Leave sts for left side and back on length of yarn or st holder.

RIGHT FRONT
Rejoin wool at armhole edge.
Next row: P2 tog, work to end of row.
Cont to work in patt from chart, dec 1 st at each end of work until 32 sts rem.
Dec at front edge until 25 sts rem.
Row 162: Cast off 8 sts, work to end of row.
Work 1 row.
Row 164: Cast off 8 sts, work to end of row.
Work 1 row.
Row 166: Cast off 9 sts.

LEFT FRONT
Remove 48 sts for left front from yarn or st holder, rejoin yarn and work to match right front, reversing all shapings.

BACK
Remove rem sts from yarn or st holder.

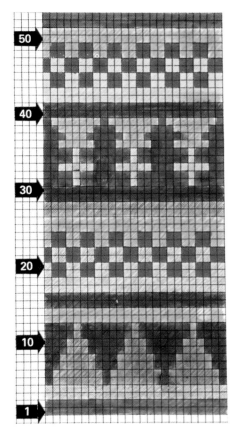

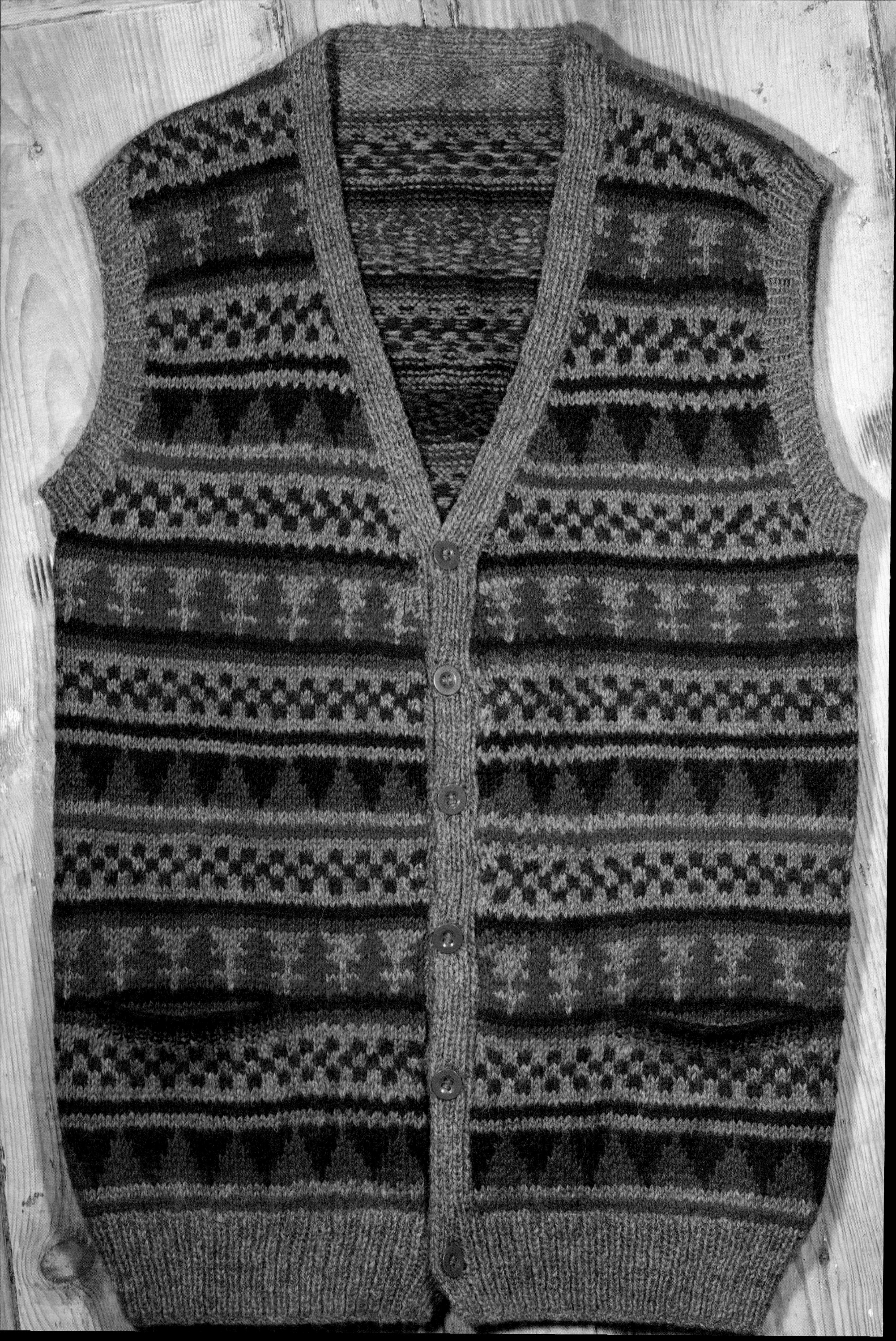

Rejoin yarn, inside of work facing.
Next row: P.
Next row and each alt row: K2 tog at each end of work 7 times (87 sts). Work without shaping on these sts until 160 rows have been completed. Cast off 8 sts at beg of next 4 rows. Cast off rem sts.

ARMBANDS (both alike)
With 3¼mm needles and main colour (olive) pick up 94[112] sts round armholes. K1, P1 rib for 2.5cm. Cast off in rib.
Sew back and front shoulders tog making a flat seam at rib.

BUTTONBAND
Left side: With 3¾mm needles, rem 7 sts from safety pin, rejoin yarn at inside edge of band.
Next row: Inc 1 st, rib to end.
Work 4 more buttonholes as before, evenly spaced so that the last is placed at the 1st dec row of front shaping. Cont band so that it reaches all round edge and down right side to bottom of rib. Stretch slightly for a firm edge. Do not cast off – leave sts on safety pin. Sew band to waistcoat stretching slightly; cast off sts on safety pin when band fits.

TO MAKE UP
Complete sewing up. Sew buttons in place. Oversew pocket linings in place on inside of work. Iron under damp cloth, except ribbing.

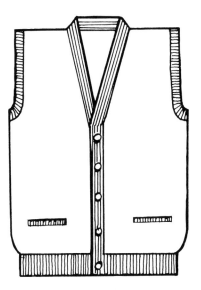

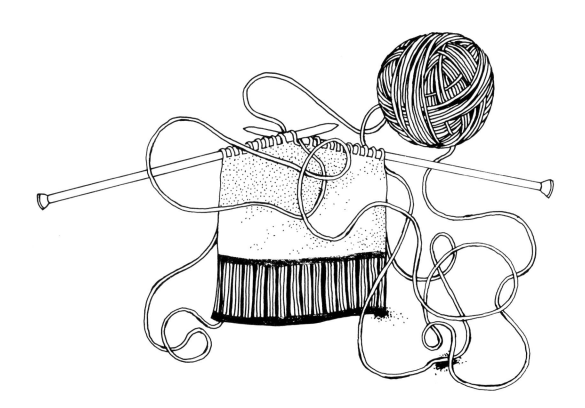

Gardener's Garters legwarmers

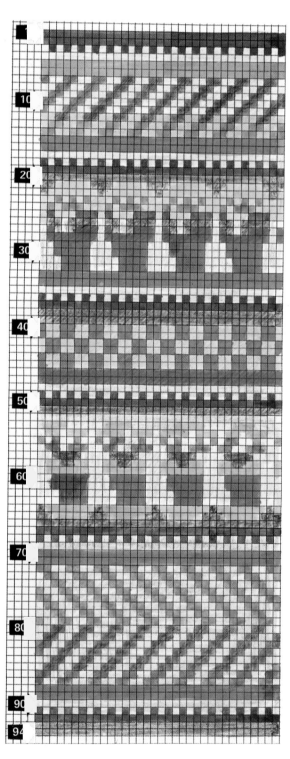

Pattern repeat 8 sts and 94 rows

Note

These legwarmers are made from double knitting wool, but as only 25g of each of the contrast colours are needed, skeins of 4 ply tapestry wool or oddments of wool left over from other work could be used and the pattern bands made up in colours of your choice.

Measurements

Length 56cm (22in).
Round calf 31cm (12in).

Materials

100g double knitting wool in main colour (beige).
25g double knitting wool in each of 9 contrast colours (navy, terracotta, mustard, dark green, olive green, bright green, ochre, red, bright yellow).
Pair 3¾mm (No 9) needles.
Pair 3mm (No 11) needles.

Tension

25 sts and 27 rows to 10cm (4in) over patt worked on 3¾mm needles.

With 3mm needles and 1st contrast (navy) cast on 79 sts.
Row 1: *K2, P2, rep from * to last 3 sts, K3.
Row 2: P3, *P2, K2, rep from * to end of row.
Repeat row 1.
Change to 2nd contrast (terracotta), work 3 more rows in rib.
Change to 3rd contrast (mustard), work 3 more rows in rib.
Change to main colour (beige), cont to rib until work measures 12cm (4¾in), inc 3 sts evenly along last row (82 sts).
Change to 4th contrast (dark green) and work from patt on chart beg at row 1 and working without shaping to row 42.
Keeping patt correct, dec 1 st at each end of every 6th row until 68 sts rem.
Change to 3mm needles and contrast colour of your choice.
Work in K2, P2 rib for 5cm (2in).
Change to 2nd contrast (terracotta), work 3 more rows in rib.
Change to 5th contrast (olive green), work 3 more rows in rib.
Cast off.

TO MAKE UP

Sew ribbing with matching yarn making a flat seam.
Sew up rest of back seam carefully matching patt.

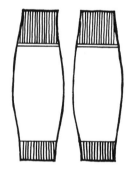

Woolly Bag

Follow back of jacket of book or endpapers for patt chart

Size

Bag:
Width 27cm (10½in).
Length 34.5cm (13½in).
Handle:
Length 71cm (28in).
Width: 3.5cm (1½in).

Materials

Small balls (½oz or less) of Shetland 2 ply in 15 contrast colours of your choice.
No 11 circular needle 46cm (18in) long.
76 × 25cm (30 × 10in) of cotton velvet or other firm washable material.
76 × 30cm (30 × 12in) of heavy Vilene or preshrunk calico.
Cotton or silk to same measurements for lining.

Tension

28 sts and 32 rows to 10cm (4in) over patt worked on No 11 needle.

BAG

With No 11 circular needle and 1st contrast at beg of design, cast on 160 sts.
Work 1 K row, 1 P row, 1 K row.
4th row: Join both ends tog to make a circle taking care that knitting is not twisted.
Cont with patt on chart working round in K only, to last row of design. K4 rows with colour on needle.
Cast off.

TO MAKE UP

Turn work inside out. Oversew bottom edges of bag tog.
Iron carefully under a damp cloth. Turn to right side.
While there is still moisture in the wool, run the iron down both side edges of bag to remove creases.

LININGS

Cut interlining and lining to measurements given for bag remembering to make a seam allowance.
Lay 1st interlining flat on table. Place 1st lining evenly over it.
Tack tog. Repeat for 2nd lining.
Lay 2nd lining over 1st, tack right through tog.
Sew down left side, across bottom edge, up right side of linings.
Remove 2nd tacking threads so that the bag now opens.
Trim interlining to seam.
Slip lining into bag, push and pull about so that the knitted design lies well on the lining.
Tack bottom edges tog through all material again. The lining will be longer than the knitting.
Tack them tog around bag opening about 2.5cm (1½in) from top.
Cut a length of velvet 56cm (22in) long × 14cm (5½in) wide.
Measure circumference of bag. Seam side seams of band to match.
Tack it to the knitted edge. Sew tog.
Tack down on outside of work.
Fold velvet band over lining and into bag. Tack edge.
Hem st band to lining on inside of work.

HANDLE

Cut length of velvet 80cm (31½in) long × 9cm (3½in) wide.

Inside of work

Tack 2 long sides tog. Sew up, remove tacking threads.
Reverse by pushing a large safety pin secured to one end of tube through to the other end, pulling the material with it so that the right side of work finally appears.
Flatten, tack. Sew 5mm (¼in) hem along both sides of handle edge.

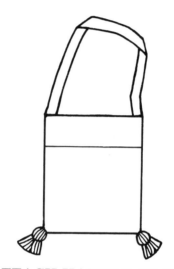

ATTACH HANDLE TO BAG

Place each end of handle at corners of opening 2cm (1¼in) in from bag edge. Adjust measurement to match finished work.
Hand-sew, turning in a small hem at rough end of material.
Hem 5mm (¼in) round edge of bag taking in both handles.
Remove all tacking threads.

TASSELS

Make 6 tassels as shown in Techniques. Sew 3 to each bottom corner of bag.

TO STRETCH

Place a book (this one is the right size) inside bag.
Hang the bag over a straight-backed chair, the handle stretched out horizontally so that the weight is evenly balanced. Leave to settle.
From time to time pull the tassels gently inwards so that the base of the bag forms a slight crescent.

WASHING INSTRUCTIONS

Hand wash, spin dry, lay flat.
When dry, making sure that the inside is *very* dry, put book in bag and hang up to settle as before.

Techniques

INTRODUCTION

All the patterns in this book are based on fairly simple shapes and equally simple techniques. It is the use of colour in the small repeating patterns that gives the garments their originality.

Once you have learnt and mastered the few basic techniques given in this chapter you will be able to make any of the numerous eye-catching jerseys, pullovers, waistcoats and cardigans given throughout the book.

If you are already an experienced knitter you may be able to pick up some tips on improving your finishing and making up of a garment, which can be as important as the actual knitting.

SECTION 1
ABBREVIATIONS, NOTES, SIZES AND NEEDLES

General abbreviations

alt	–	alternate(ly)
beg	–	begin(ning)
ch	–	chains
cm	–	centimetres
cont	–	continu(e)(ing)
dc	–	double crochet
dec	–	decrease(ing)
foll	–	follow(ing)
g st	–	garter stitch
inc	–	increase(ing)
K	–	knit
mm	–	millimetre(s)
patt	–	pattern
psso	–	pass slipped stitch over
P	–	purl
rem	–	remain(ing)
rep	–	repeat(ing)
sl	–	slip
st(s)	–	stitch(es)
st st	–	stocking stitch
tog	–	together
yfwd	–	yarn forward
yrh	–	yarn round hook

Notes

If there is a heading called 'notes' at the beginning of a pattern it is to call your attention to some special point within the pattern. Always take care to read it carefully as mistakes are not always easy to correct.

Sizes and tension

Most patterns are given in a choice of sizes. Instructions are usually given for the smallest size with the larger sizes given in brackets in ascending order.

The final size of your garment will depend on whether the knitting has been worked to the correct tension. At the beginning of every pattern there is always a section to tell you how many stitches and rows should be worked to 10cm (4in). It is important that you work a tension square first and if necessary use a different size pair of needles to obtain the correct tension. Half a stitch out over the tension square could mean the finished garment being several centimetres too big or too small.

Needle sizes

Most needles these days are sold in millimetre (mm) sizes and most patterns tell you the correct metric size to buy.

If you wish to knit from an old pattern or use old needles which still quote imperial sizes use the chart below to find their equivalent metric size.

Metric	Imperial
2mm	14
2¼mm	13
2¾mm	12
3mm	11
3¼mm	10
3¾mm	9
4mm	8
4½mm	7
5mm	6
5½mm	5
6mm	4
6½mm	3
7mm	2
7½mm	1
8mm	0
9mm	00
10mm	000

Circular needles

Circular needles are two double-ended needles joined by a flexible length of plastic. Instructions for their use are usually provided with the packing when you buy them.

They are available in several different lengths from 40 to 100cm (15¾ to 39in). In many ways knitting with circular needles is an ideal answer for those who dislike making up, or find it difficult to follow a graph for a purl row. Use them when there are too many stitches to hold on a normal straight needle – eg for Strawberries waistcoat or one of the other waistcoats which could be knitted in one piece.

Adapting patterns for use with circular needles

Pullovers and jumpers

Add together the number of stitches for front and back and work the rib in a complete circle. Remember to work to and fro for the first few rows. as otherwise the work is liable to twist round the needles. On the first row of pattern, mark the beginning of the row with a contrast-coloured length of wool – slip it over the needle and pass it from one point to the other at the end of the row. Remember to increase evenly as given in the instructions.

When the armholes are reached, the knitting will have to be worked to and fro in the usual way. Finish and make up the garment, weaving in the ends and making sure that there is no uneven pulling.

Unfortunately sleeves cannot be knitted in this way on circular needles as they are too narrow. They can, however, be worked on a set of double-pointed needles.

SECTION 2
BASIC CASTING ON, KNIT AND PURL STITCHES AND CASTING OFF

Casting on

1 Make a slip loop in the end of a ball of yarn and place on to a knitting needle. Hold this needle in your left hand. Take hold of the yarn between the slip loop and the ball in your right hand and wind it once round your little finger. Take the yarn underneath the middle two fingers and then up and over your first (index) finger.

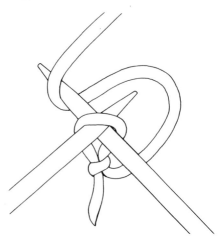

Practise picking up the yarn as described so that there is about 3cm of yarn between the slip loop on the left-hand needle and the yarn passing over your right-hand index finger. Pull this yarn fairly taut; this is what controls the tension of your knitting. Place the second needle in your right hand. Push the right-hand needle through the loop on the left-hand needle. Take the yarn under and back over the top of the right-hand needle.
2 With the right-hand needle, draw a loop through. Place this stitch on to the left-hand needle.

3 Insert the right-hand needle between the two stitches on the left-hand needle.

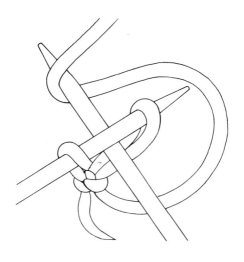

Take the yarn under and back over the top of the right-hand needle and draw a loop through. Place this stitch on to the left-hand needle. Repeat this step until the required number of stitches are on the needle.

The knit stitch

1 Keeping the yarn to the right of the right-hand needle (or to the back of the work), insert the right-hand needle from front to back in the first stitch on the left-hand needle. Take the yarn under and back over the right-hand needle.

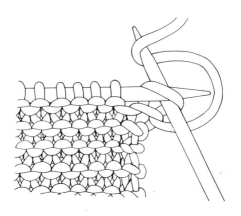

2 Draw a loop through. Leave new stitch on right-hand needle, drop old stitch off left-hand needle. Repeat these two steps to end of row.

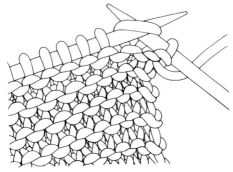

The purl stitch

1 Keeping yarn at the front of the work, insert needle from right to left into the first stitch on the left-hand needle.

Take the yarn across in front, over the top, then back round under the right-hand needle.

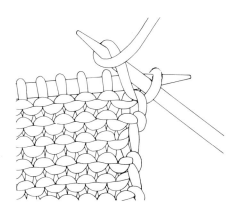

2 Draw a loop through. Leave new stitch on right-hand needle, drop old stitch off right-hand needle. Repeat these two steps to end of row.

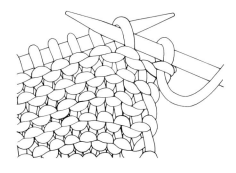

Garter stitch and stocking stitch

Garter stitch is formed by knitting or purling every row.

Stocking stitch is formed by alternately knitting a row then purling a row.

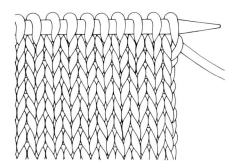

Casting off

1 Knit the first two stitches of the row. With the point of the left-hand needle lift the first stitch knitted on

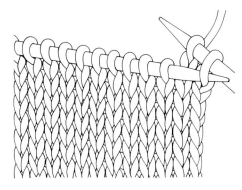

the right-hand needle over the second stitch and off the needle.

2 Knit the next stitch, then repeat step 1 until only one stitch remains. Break off the yarn and thread through last stitch to fasten off.

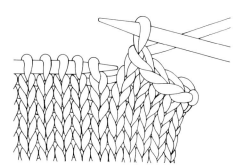

SECTION 3
RIBBING, INCREASING AND DECREASING

Ribbing

Ribbing is formed by working a regular sequence of knit and purl stitches. It has an elasticity which is ideal for holding a jersey in shape at the welt, cuffs and neckband where they can become easily stretched.

The most common form is single rib which is worked by alternately knitting and purling the stitches along the row as shown in the drawing.

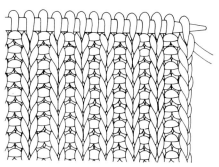

On the next row, knit all the purl stitches of the previous row and purl all the knit stitches. Other ribs are formed by knitting two then purling two, or three and three.

To cast off ribbing with a neat but elastic edge, knit every knit stitch and purl every purl stitch before lifting the previous stitch over. For a rather unusual finish change to a contrast colour from the main ribbing and cast off by knitting every stitch.

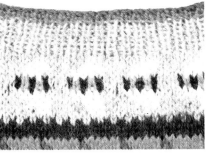

Increasing

Increasing is needed when shaping a garment. If several stitches are needed all at once, just cast on the required number at the beginning of the row.

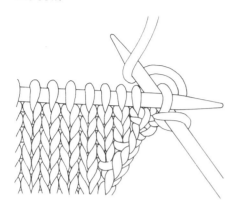

If only one stitch at a time is needed to form gradual increases, then work them by knitting into the front and back of a stitch as follows:

With the right-hand needle knit into the stitch in the normal way, but do not let the old stitch drop off the needle.

Take the right-hand needle round to the back of the stitch, insert the needle through the back loop of the stitch and draw through a loop. There are now two stitches on the right-hand needle. Let the old stitch drop off the left-hand needle.

Decreasing

Decreasing, as with increasing, is used when shaping a garment. If several stitches need to be decreased all at once, just cast off the required number at the beginning or end of the row. If only one stitch needs to be decreased, just knit two stitches together as follows:

Work to the position for the decrease. Insert the right-hand needle from front to back through both of the next two stitches (at the same time). Continue knitting the stitch in the normal way allowing both of the stitches to drop off the left-hand needle.

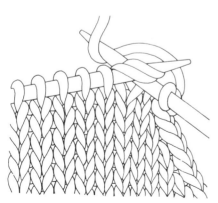

SECTION 4
COLOUR WORK

Working in two or more colours

When working in two or more colours in a row it is sometimes very difficult to ensure that you do not pull the yarns not in use too tightly or leave them hanging too loosely at the back of the work. The best way to solve this when carrying yarn over three or more stitches is to weave the yarns in whilst knitting.

1 On a knit row, hold the yarn that is being carried in the left hand. Insert the right-hand needle into the stitch from front to back. Hook the yarn in the left hand over the top of the right-hand needle, then continue to knit the stitch in the normal way.
Repeat this on every alternate stitch until you change yarns.

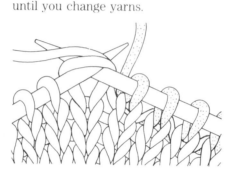

2 On a purl row, hold the yarn to be carried in the left hand. Insert the right-hand needle into the next stitch from right to left. Hook the yarn in the left hand up over the right-hand needle, then continue to purl the stitch in the normal way.
Repeat this on every alternate stitch until you change yarns.

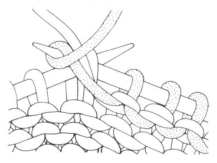

Working from charts

All the patterns in this book are given in chart form.
Each row of squares represents one row of knitting and each individual square represents one stitch to be knitted in whichever colour it is shown in.
Unless otherwise quoted in the pattern all right-side rows are generally read from right to left on the chart and all wrong-side rows from left to right.

SECTION 5
BUTTONHOLES, TASSELS, POMPONS AND CORDS

Buttonholes

There are two methods of working buttonholes. The first is to work them at the same time as knitting the buttonhole border by casting off and casting on a set number of stitches, while the second is to add them to the finished garment by making a loop with matching yarn and working buttonhole stitch over it.

Knitted buttonholes

Work in rib (or pattern) to position for first buttonhole. Cast off enough stitches to allow the button through, then continue working in pattern to the position for the next buttonhole. On the next row work to the first set of cast-off stitches. Turn the work and cast on the same number of stitches that were cast off on the previous row. Turn the work again and continue in pattern to the next buttonhole.

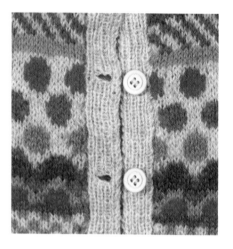

If only a small buttonhole is needed as on baby garments, a simpler method is to work to the position for the first buttonhole, bring the yarn forward to form a hole, then work the next two stitches together. This method works the buttonholes all in one row.

Button loops

Cut a length of matching yarn and thread into a needle. Join yarn at position of first buttonhole at edge of buttonhole border and take a small stitch. Leave a space along the edge just a little less than the width of the button, then make another small stitch, allowing the length of yarn for the loop to lie loosely along edge of garment. Go back and take another small stitch at the beginning of the loop.

Repeat this twice more so that there are four thicknesses of yarn for the loop.
Now, working over all four thicknesses, neaten the loop with buttonhole stitch.

Tassels

1 Cut a piece of card the depth of the tassel required. Wind yarn round and round the card to obtain the required size of tassel. Tie another piece of yarn round the threads at the top of the card and fasten securely leaving an end approximately 20cm long.
Cut the threads at the lower edge of card.

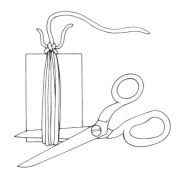

2 Wind the long end of yarn round the top of the tassel to form a neat shank.
Thread this end into a needle. Bring the end of yarn up through the centre of the tassel and out through the top.

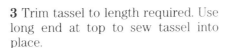

3 Trim tassel to length required. Use long end at top to sew tassel into place.

Pompons

1 Cut two circles of card the size of the required pompon. Cut out a central hole about one quarter to one third the size of the circles.
Take a length of yarn and wind it over and over the card until the central hole is almost full. It is sometimes better to thread a needle with the yarn for winding, as this makes it easier to pass it through the hole.

2 With a pair of sharp scissors cut the yarn right round the edges of the circle, passing the blade of the scissors between the two cardboard circles. Take a length of yarn and tie securely round the centre of the pompon.

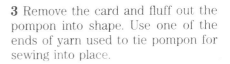

3 Remove the card and fluff out the pompon into shape. Use one of the ends of yarn used to tie pompon for sewing into place.

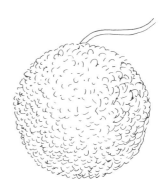

Twisted cords

A twisted cord is a very quick and simple way to make a tie or drawstring for a garment.
First work out the length and thickness that you want the finished cord to be.
It is better to make them from only two, three or four thicknesses of yarn.
Cut off the chosen number of lengths approximately three times the required finished length.
Make a slip knot in both ends and slip a pencil through each.
Twist each pencil in opposite directions until you cannot twist the yarn any more without knots forming.
Fold the twisted cord in half by holding the two ends together with one hand, whilst holding the folded end with the other, keeping the yarn held taut.
Now let go of the folded end and the two halves of yarn will twist round each other.
Tie a knot in each end of the cord to secure.
If an extra long length of cord is needed either ask someone to hold the other end for you or tie it to a door handle.

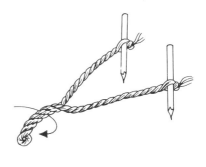

SECTION 6
BLOCKING, PRESSING, MAKING UP AND GRAFTING

Blocking

For a really professional finish block all pieces of knitting before making up.

First check the sizes that the pieces should be.

If you do not have a blocking board, a thick layer of blanket covered with an old sheet spread out on a table top will do.

Pin out all pieces to the sizes given, except for any ribbing.

If the yarn cannot be pressed or the knitting is in a textured stitch which could be spoilt, then dampen all the pieces with a light spray of water and leave in position until completely dry.

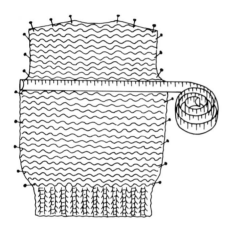

Pressing

If, once the pieces have been blocked, you are required to press the pieces then check with the ballband on the yarn whether you should use a dry or damp cloth. Cover each piece with a cloth and very gently press into shape.

If using steam, make sure the knitting is completely dry before removing from the blocking board.

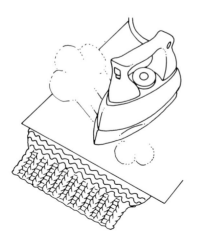

Making up

The instructions in the pattern will usually tell you the order in which to assemble the pieces.

The neatest and easiest way to seam the edges together is to use back-stitch, easing seams together and matching stripes and patterns as you work.

For ribbing, a plain oversewn seam is usually best, allowing the rib to lie flat.

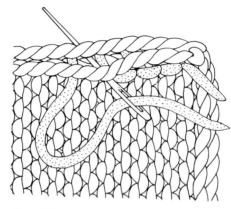

Grafting

A very neat way of joining two pieces of knitting together is by grafting.

If this technique is carried out correctly, the join will not show.

Leave both pieces of knitting on the needles until the very last minute, making sure that there is the same number of stitches on both the pieces to be joined.

If the yarn can be pressed, very lightly press the stitches that are on the needle to set them, this will help to stop them unravelling.

Remove the needles and place both pieces of knitting on to a flat surface with the open stitches facing each other.

Thread a needle with a length of matching yarn (about four times the width of the pieces of knitting) and working backwards and forwards from one set of stitches to the other gradually join the two pieces of knitting, imitating the knitted stitches.

SECTION 7
CROCHET CORDS AND EDGES

Crochet is a quick and easy way of making cords for tying or neatening edges. Two very basic stitches are all that are needed.

Holding yarn and hook

Make a slip loop in the end of a ball of yarn and place on crochet hook.

Hold the crochet hook in the right hand, wind yarn round the little finger of your left hand and over middle two fingers as shown in diagram.

The work is held between thumb and first finger of left hand.

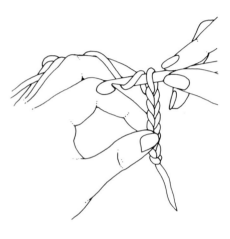

Chain

Take hook (in right hand) under and over yarn. Draw yarn through loop on hook. This is one chain formed.

Repeat until chain is as long as required.

Double crochet edging

Join yarn to right-hand corner of edge to be neatened. Hold hook and yarn as given above.

Insert hook into first stitch at corner, yarn round hook and draw a loop through (one loop on hook).

*Insert hook into next stitch along knitting, yarn round hook and draw a

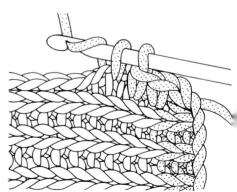

loop through (two loops now on hook), yarn round hook again and draw through two loops on hook (one loop on hook).

Repeat from * to end of edge to be neatened.

This method is used throughout the patterns in the book where one or two rows are worked in a contrast on the ribbing at the welt and centre front borders to link up the colours at the side edge of the front borders.

SECTION 8
CARE OF KNITWEAR

Once you have taken time and trouble to knit, block, press and make up your garment it is a pity to spoil it later on by incorrect washing and drying.

Most yarn that you buy comes with ballbands or labels with instructions on washing and caring for your garment.

These should be noted down at the time of knitting so that they do not get mislaid. If the yarn does not have a label or any washing instructions, then contact the manufacturers to find out what they recommend.

If in doubt, hand wash only in warm water (maximum 30°C), gently squeeze excess water out and then dry flat. This is best done by placing on a piece of old towel, pulling into shape, then leaving until completely dry.

More Knitting Know-How

Sizing up

The garments in this book start off very small because it is most important for a new baby to have something pretty to wear on arrival. Progressively through the book, the garments are larger. Measurements are given for them all, but of course children come in all shapes and sizes. Remember too how quickly they grow, and that teenagers seem to like their clothes either very tight or very baggy. Why not measure an existing garment which suits particularly well, and see whether there is a pattern in the book which corresponds to it.

No attempt has been made to divide the designs into boys' or girls', or men's or women's – it is so much a matter of personal taste. Some young men love Sissy Pink, for example; others wouldn't be seen dead in it! If you prefer, you can reverse the buttonhole band on any of the waistcoats depending on whether it is being knitted for a man or a woman.

Wool gathering

Most of the garments in this book are made either from Shetland 2 ply yarn (which comes in 1oz skeins and cones for machine knitting and knits up as a 4 ply) or from Shetland 3 ply yarn in 2oz skeins giving heavier duty knitwear for outdoor wear. Shetland yarn has been chosen because it was created to be worked in traditional Fair Isle patterns and gives a 'soft edge' to the frequent colour changes. There are plenty of good stockists almost everywhere, but if you have any difficulties, the main mail order supplier is Jamieson & Smith (SWB) Ltd, 90 North Road, Lerwick, Shetland Isles ZE1 0PQ, who will supply you with shade cards.

Other yarns can be substituted. Double knitting knits up very much the same as Shetland 3 ply, and cotton or even some mixtures could be used instead. It is fun to work mohair into some of the designs such as the Bunny Rabbits jumper on page 42. Whenever a substitute yarn is used, it is essential to knit a tension swatch using the needles given, and adjust the needle size as necessary.

Gardener's Garters (page 98) and Flowerpots (page 90) have been made up in double knitting, while Comets is a mixture of double knitting and 4 ply tapestry wool. Tapestry wool, like Shetland, comes in a very wide range of colours and works well with double knitting. This is particularly useful when only small amounts of different colours are needed as it comes in 15yd skeins.

Dyeing your own yarn

Pure wool takes to dyeing very well indeed. Natural undyed wool is, of course, the best basis for your dyeing, but ready-dyed wool can also be used. A light coloured yarn which you are not happy with – perhaps because it is too bright – can be changed; for example, turquoise with a wash of yellow ochre makes a lovely green.

One advantage of using hand-dyed wool in Fair Isle type knitting is that the small amounts needed for each colour can easily be managed in an average kitchen pot – impossible when producing large amounts for a large single-coloured garment.

There are two methods which can be used. The first is simply to buy commercial dyes. Follow the instructions for wool very carefully, using either the hot water or cold water method. Remember to tie up the hanks of wool in several places – but not tightly – so that they don't get tangled when you stir them round in the pot.

The second method is to make your own vegetable or animal dyes. Study the books in your local Public Library or bookshop. It is very important to mix the right amount of mordants together with the dye so that the colour remains fixed. The countryside will provide berries, bark and lichen. Onions and other garden vegetables and flowers too give beautiful soft greens, yellows and purples. Animal dyes such as dried cochineal produce reds. Dip a small piece of wool into the dye pot on the stove to test how it will look – remembering that it will actually dry lighter.

Many hands make bright work

It's quite likely that there are many garments in this book which you'd love to have or give as presents to family and friends, but simply haven't the time to knit yourself. Don't despair. Put a small ad in your local paper or craft magazine – you will be surprised how many willing helpers come forward. Handwork takes time, but a housebound knitter who can pick up the work at odd moments of the day gets through a surprising amount of work – and at a very reasonable cost to you when compared to a similar shop-bought garment. Finding fellow-knitters is rewarding in other ways too. You discuss new ideas and make new friends. I know.

Converting patterns for machine knitting

Most of the garments in this book can easily be made on any of the modern punchcard knitting machines.

The basic know-how on how to use your machine is given in your instruction manual together with how to work increasing, decreasing, ribbing etc.

The only additional help you will need is how to convert the hand-knitting charts given with each pattern so that they can be punched on to a blank card suitable for your machine.

Choosing the design

First of all choose the design that you wish to knit and check that each small section of pattern on the chart will divide into the number of stitches covered by the punchcard on your machine.

Most machines have punchcards that go over 24 stitches, which is suitable for 2, 4, 6, 8, 12 and 24 stitch pattern repeats.

Adapting the pattern

If you find the design you wish to use has a section of pattern which is, for example, a seven stitch pattern repeat as in the 'darts' pattern, it is sometimes possible to alter either all of the pattern or just the part which is wrong very slightly without spoiling the overall effect.

Punching the card

Before beginning to punch the card, check the chart and see which colours have been used most and use these as the background colours to go through the main yarn feeder, then go through and mark the holes which correspond with the contrast colour to go through the secondary yarn feeder.

Now punch the marked holes.

For the 'oranges and lemons' pattern, as illustrated, you would now knit as follows:

2 rows colour A in yarn feed 1.

4 sts

6 sts

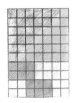

7 sts

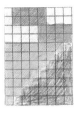

8 sts

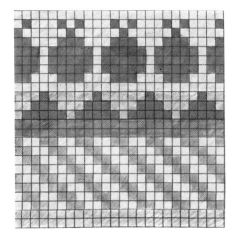

24 sts

2 rows colour B in yarn feed 1.
8 rows C in yarn feed 1 and D in yarn feed 2.
2 rows A in yarn feed 1.
3 rows B in yarn feed 1 and E in yarn feed 2.
1 row C in yarn feed 1.
5 rows C in yarn feed 1 and F in yarn feed 2.
2 rows C in yarn feed 1 and E in yarn feed 2.
1 row C in yarn feed 1.

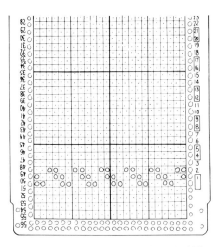

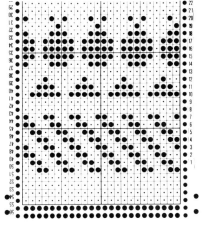

Working three colours in a row

If you need to work a third colour into some of the pattern rows this can be done as follows:

Punch the card as given above, but do not punch a hole where the third colour is to be knitted.

Work in pattern to the row that has three colours, then push every needle which represents the stitch to be knitted in the third colour forward into holding position and set the machine so that it does not knit these stitches. Knit the row with the main and first contrast colours as usual.

Join in the second contrast colour and knit the stitches that are on the needles in holding position back into working position manually, taking care to keep the same tension. Repeat this process on every row with an extra colour.

Designing your own knitwear

Getting started

A squared exercise book or graph pad (or use the graph paper printed at the end of this book), a few felt pens and coloured pencils are all you need to start with.

Choose the motifs in this book which you like best, and copy from the charts on to your graph paper in colour. It's a good idea to leave a space between each row of motifs so that you can cut out the rows and then place them in various combinations for the best effect; finally stick them all together to create the overall design. Number each row and count up how many colours are needed.

If you are a beginner, don't rush out and buy lots of wool and different sized needles. A pair of medium size needles such as 3¼mm (No 10) and oddments of wool from friends or remnant sales will do. Tapestry wool comes in skeins of 15 yards or so; 5 or 6 different colours of your choice will give you a good start.

Take up your needle and cast on about 24 sts, work a few rows in stocking stitch and then start the pattern. Work from your graph changing any colour or pattern which you are not happy with. Cast off. Now you are a designer.

And do not stop here. Design your own motifs using the graph paper provided, intersperse them with others you like from the book and so produce a truly original design. The Swifts design on the facing page is an example of what you can achieve.

Next, decide what garment you are going to make.

Basic V neck pullover

If you decide to make a V neck pullover, base your garment on a design in the book such as Checkers. Look up the total number of stitches used on the first pattern row. Let's suppose there are a total of 114 sts and a pattern with an 8 st repeat is being used. The sum is as follows:

$$114 \div 8 = 14 + 2$$

So the pattern can be repeated 14 times and as there are 2 stitches left over, an extra stitch should be worked at each end of each row. This stitch will be sewn into the seam. Sometimes the sum is not quite so easy:

$$eg \ 120 \div 8 = 15 + 5$$

When this happens a little more thought about the pattern is re-

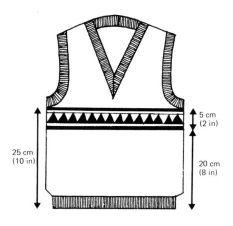

quired. It may be possible to have half a pattern at the end of the row on the front and the other half continued on the back of the pullover. If this does not work, then 3 stitches can be knitted at the beginning of the row and 2 at the end.

A pattern, or part of a pattern, can be used just under the arms as a strip round the chest/bust.

This again requires a simple calculation. Under the heading 'Tension' you are told how many rows of pattern there are to 10cm (4in), so once you know how many cm (in) deep your chosen pattern is, you can simply deduct this from the total underarm measurement; ie if the pattern is 5cm (2in) deep and the total underarm measurement is 25cm (10in), knit 20cm (8in) and then work your pattern, ending with 2 rows in the main colour again

before decreasing for the armholes.

If you are designing a V neck pullover with an allover pattern, it is a good idea to copy out one of the diagrams given for a V neck from the book – taking care to place the motif (eg Mushrooms) evenly on each side of the decreasing for the V. One of the advantages of designing your own work is that you can take up another colour or pattern just as the mood takes you, creating something original as you go along.

How to work your own allover design

1 Make sure that the motif you choose is simple and not more than 10 stitches wide.

2 When making your graph, place the motif in the centre and work outwards towards the edges at first. Alternatively, place the motifs so that they fall evenly either side of the centre of the front.

3 Provided that the allover design looks good, do not worry about exactly matching the motifs on the front and back at the side seam. These swifts, for example, do not always match up precisely when incorporated in basic 6 or 8 pattern repeats. A certain irregularity often adds interest to a garment.

4 This pattern could also be used for edging bands on an otherwise plain jumper, or for a band across the front and back of a plain pullover.

Borders

Here are a few simple borders for you to use. Several of the other patterns in the book can be adapted in the same way for use as bands. Remember that the two-colour knitting is a different tension from the plain one-colour knitting. Working the two-colour pattern on 3¼mm (No 10) needles and the one-colour background on 3mm (No 11) needles will balance the overall look and texture of the garment.

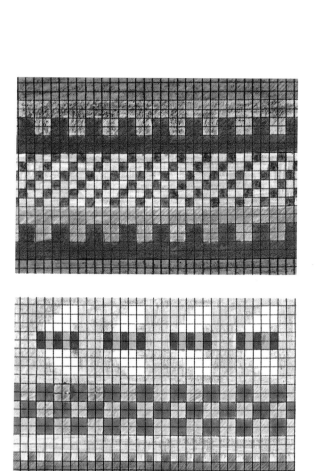

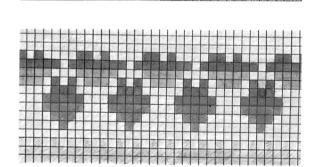

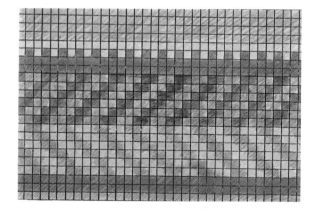

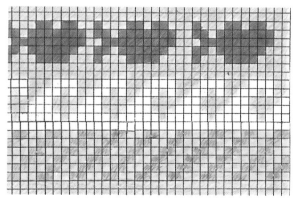

Colouring in

Pretend you are at nursery school again . . .

The patterns on the next few pages of graph paper await your colouring pens; the plain graph paper following them gives you the opportunity to start from scratch. You will probably prefer to have the pages photocopied, but you can of course work directly on the pages here.

Start colouring in. Let yourself go. Try all sorts of combinations – day and night, summer and autumn, sun and mist, seaside and garden. The effect of using predominantly bright or pastel colours will often surprise you, giving an entirely different impression from the same design, and you will find that shades you never dreamed of putting together can work well.

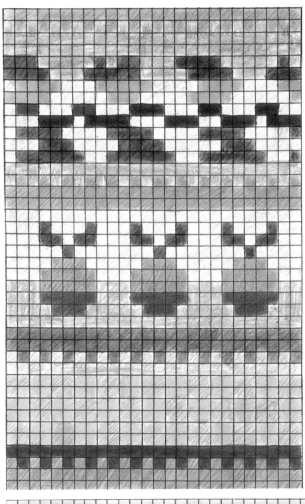

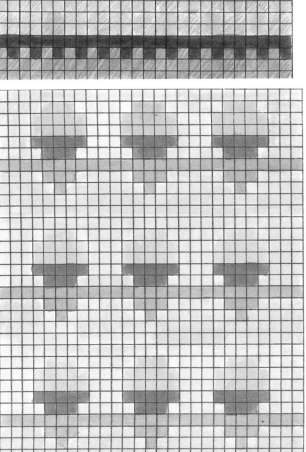

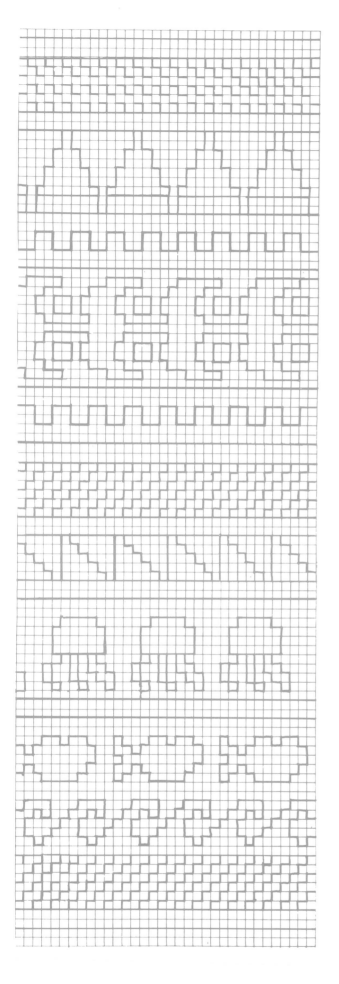

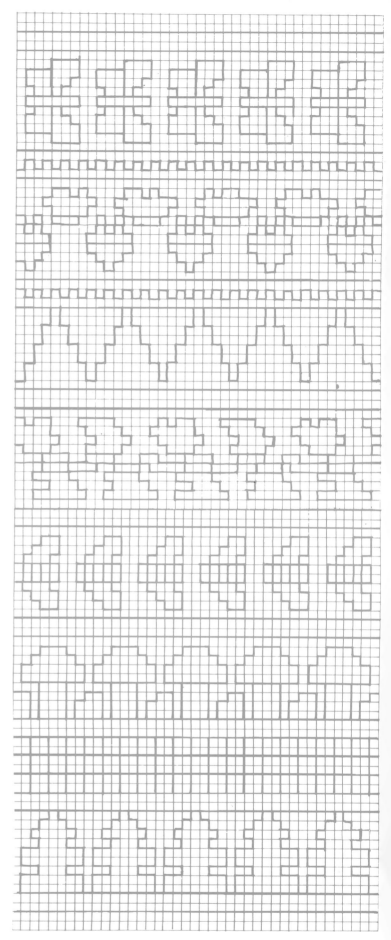

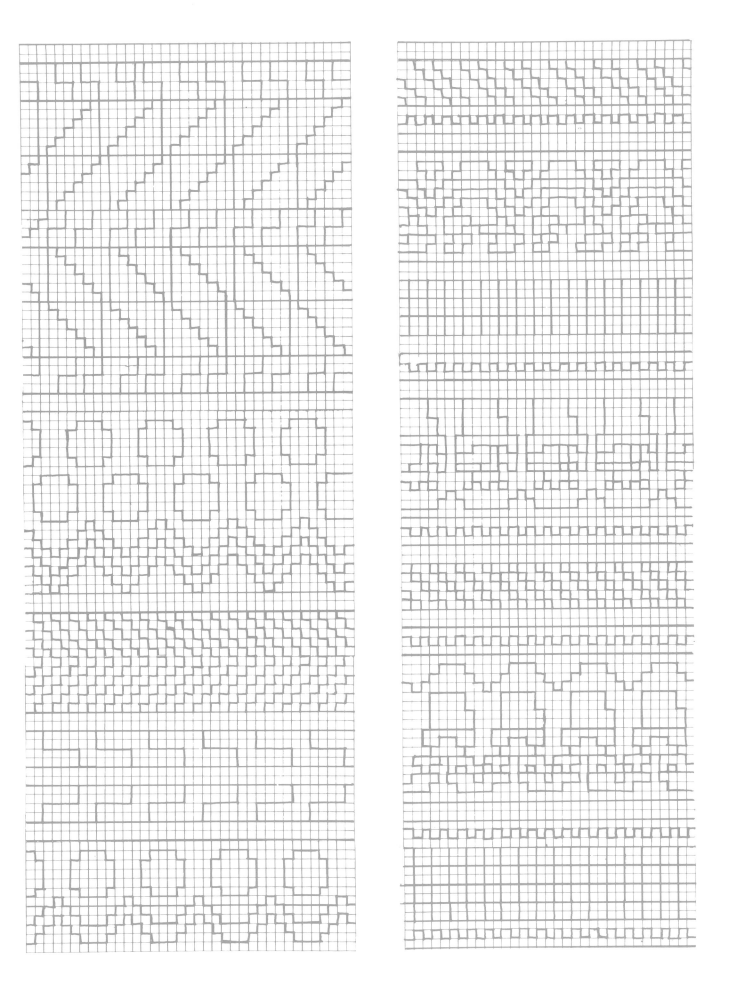

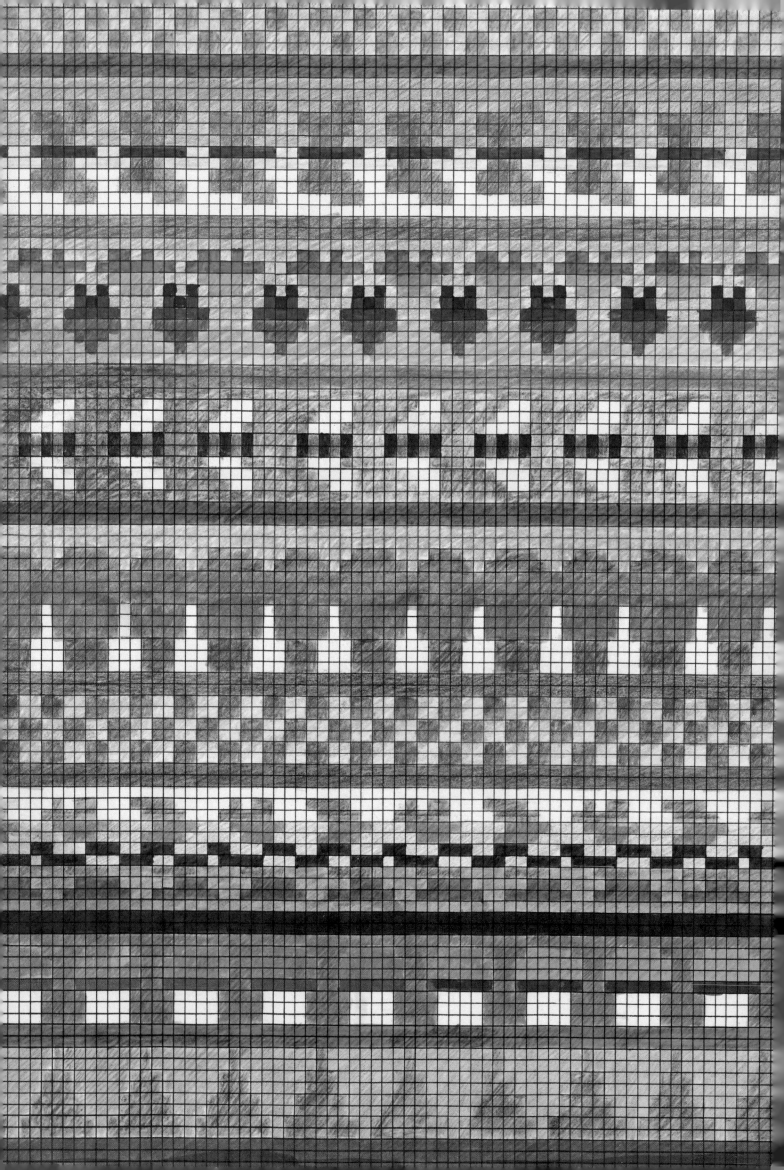